GREEK

Phrase Book & Dictionary

D1016112

HarperCollins*Publishers*

Consultants: Translexis Ltd

SuperGreek font supplied by Linguist's Software Inc.

First published 1990
Copyright © HarperCollins Publishers
Reprint 10 8 8 7 6 5 4
Printed in Italy by Amadeus SpA, Rome
ISBN 0 00-435869-4

Your *Collins Phrase Book & Dictionary* is a handy, quick-reference guide that will help you make the most of your stay abroad. Its clear layout, with direct alphabetical access to the relevant information, will save you valuable time when you need that crucial word or phrase.

There are two main sections in this book:

• 70 practical topics arranged in A-Z order from **ACCIDENTS** to **WINTER SPORTS** via such subjects as **MENUS**, **ROOM SERVICE** and **TAXIS**. Each topic gives you the basic phrases you will need along with clear but simple pronunciation guidelines. In many cases, there's the added bonus of our 'Streetwise' travel tips – practical and often invaluable travel information.

And, if you've found the right phrase but still need a vital word, you're sure to find it in the final topic, **WORDS**, a brief but rigorously practical list of English words and their translations, chosen for their relevance to the needs of the general traveller.

• A 2000-word foreign vocabulary; the key to all those mystifying but important notices, traffic signs, menus, etc which confront the traveller at every turn. This mini-dictionary will help you enjoy to the full the country's cuisine, save you time when asking directions, and perhaps prevent you getting into one or two tricky situations!

So, just flick through the pages to find the information you require. Why not start with a quick look at the **GRAMMAR**, **ALPHABET** and **PRONUNCIATION** topics? From there on the going is easy with your *Collins Phrase Book & Dictionary*.

Καλο ταξιδι!

LIST OF TOPICS

Streetwise

You should carry with you a valid British driving licence, or an international driving permit, and your vehicle registration certificate. Third-party insurance is essential and this is best carried in the form of an international Green Card which you should obtain from your insurers. For emergency medical assistance, dial 116.

I've crashed my car	Τρακάρισα tra**ka**-reesa
Can I see your insurance certificate please?	Μπορώ να δω την ασφάλειά σας παρακαλώ; boro na dho teen as**fa**-lee**a** sas para-ka**lo**?
We will have to report it to the police	Πρέπει να το δηλώσουμε στην αστυνομία **pre**pee na to dhee**lo**-soo-me steen astee-no**mee**-a
We should call the police	Πρέπει να καλέσουμε την αστυνομία **pre**pee na ka**le**-soo-me teen astee-no**mee**-a
He ran into me	Έπεσε επάνω μου **e**-pe-se e**pa**no moo
He was driving too fast	Έτρεχε πολύ **e**-tre-khe po**lee**
He was too close	Δεν κρατούσε απόσταση dhen kra**too**-se a**po**-stasee
He did not give way	Παραβίασε το στοπ para**vee**-a-se to stop
The car number was ...	Ο αριθμός του αυτοκινήτου ήταν ... o areeth-**mos** too afto-kee**nee**too **ee**tan ...

ACCIDENTS – INJURIES

Streetwise

Before you set off it is advisable to obtain medical insurance. Dial 166 for medical aid. Carry your passport and your E111 (or other medical insurance) form at all times.

There has been an accident	Έχει γίνει ατύχημα *ekhee yeenee atee-kheema*
Call an ambulance/ a doctor	Καλέστε ένα ασθενοφόρο/γιατρό *kales-te ena astheno-foro/yatro*
He has hurt himself	Έχει χτυπήσει *ekhee khtee-peesee*
I am hurt	Έχω χτυπήσει *ekho khtee-peesee*
He is seriously injured/bleeding	Έχει χτυπήσει σοβαρά/Χάνει πολύ αίμα *ekhee khtee-peesee sovara/khanee polee ema*
He can't breathe/ move	Δεν μπορεί να αναπνεύσει/κινηθεί *dhen boree na anapnev-see/keenee-thee*
I can't move my arm/leg	Δεν μπορώ να κουνήσω το χέρι/πόδι μου *dhen boro na koo-neeso to kheree/podhee moo*
Don't move him	Μην τον μετακινείτε *meen ton meta-keenee-te*
I have had a fall	Έπεσα *e-pesa*
Help!	Βοήθεια! *voeetheea!*

See also **EMERGENCIES**

ACCOMMODATION

Streetwise

Hotels are graded from luxury class (L) through first to fifth class (A-E).
Room prices are usually displayed on bedroom doors. Prices in most
cases are per room and a 15% service charge is normally included in
the bill. Private rooms (δωμάτια dho-**ma**teea in Greek) are available in
most resorts – enquire at the nearest taverna, or at the local Tourist
Police station.

I want to reserve a single/double room	Θέλω να κλείσω μονό/διπλό δωμάτιο **the**lo na **klee**so mo**no**/dhee**plo** dho**ma**tee-o
With bath/shower	Με μπάνιο/ντους me **ba**nee-o/doos
Do you have facilities for the disabled?	Έχετε εγκαταστάσεις για ανάπηρους; **ekh**-ete enkata-**sta**sees ya a**na**-peeroos?
I want bed and breakfast	Θέλω δωμάτιο με πρωινό **the**lo dho**ma**tee-o me pro-**ee**no
What is the daily/ weekly rate?	Πόσο την ημέρα/εβδομάδα; **po**so teen ee**me**ra/ev-dho-**ma**dha?
I want to stay three nights/from ... till ...	Θέλω να μείνω για τρεις νύχτες/από ... μέχρι ... **the**lo na **mee**no ya trees **nee**-khtes/a**po** ... **me**kh-ree ...
We'll be arriving at ...	Θα φτάσουμε στις ... tha **fta**-soo-me stees ... (see **TIME**)

See also **HOTEL DESK, ROOM SERVICE, SELF-CATERING**

AIRPORT

Streetwise

Look out for the following signs:

ΤΕΛΩΝΕΙΟ	Customs
ΟΥΔΕΝ ΠΡΟΣ ΔΗΛΩΣΗ	Nothing to Declare
ΕΙΔΗ ΠΡΟΣ ΔΗΛΩΣΗ	Goods to Declare
ΕΛΕΓΧΟΣ ΔΙΑΒΑΤΗΡΙΩΝ	Passport Control

Where do I check in for the flight to Rhodes?
Πού είναι ο έλεγχος αποσκευών για την πτήση στη Ρόδο;
poo ee-ne o elen-khos apo-skevon ya teen pteesee stee rodho?

I'd like an aisle/a window seat
Θα ήθελα θέση στο διάδρομο/σε παράθυρο
tha eethela thesee sto dhee-adhromo/se para-theero

Will a meal be served on the plane?
Θα σερβιριστεί γεύμα στο αεροπλάνο;
tha servee-reestee yevma sto aero-plano?

Where is the snack bar/duty-free shop?
Πού είναι το μπαρ/κατάστημα αφορολόγητων ειδών;
poo ee-ne to bar/kata-steema aforo-loyeeton eedhon?

Where do I get the bus to town?
Από πού μπορώ να πάρω το λεωφορείο για την πόλη;
apo poo boro na paro to leo-foree-o ya teen polee?

Where are the taxis/telephones?
Πού είναι η πιάτσα των ταξί/τα τηλέφωνα;
poo ee-ne ee pee-atsa ton taksee/ ta teele-fona?

I want to hire a car
Θέλω να νοικιάσω ένα αυτοκίνητο
thelo na neekee-aso ena afto-keeneeto

In case you want to spell anything in Greek, here are the names of the letters:

α, Α	άλφα *alfa*		ν, Ν	νι *nee*
β, Β	βήτα *veeta*		ξ, Ξ	ξι *ksee*
γ, Γ	γάμα *ghama*		ο, Ο	όμικρον *o-meekron*
δ, Δ	δέλτα *dhelta*		π, Π	πι *pee*
ε, Ε	έψιλον *ep-seelon*		ρ, Ρ	ρο *ro*
ζ, Ζ	ζήτα *zeeta*		σ, ς, Σ	σίγμα *seegh-ma*
η, Η	ήτα *eeta*		τ, Τ	ταυ *taf*
θ, Θ	θήτα *theeta*		υ, Υ	ύψιλον *eep-seelon*
ι, Ι	γιώτα *yota*		φ, Φ	φι *fee*
κ, Κ	κάπα *kapa*		χ, Χ	χι *khee*
λ, Λ	λάμδα *lam-dha*		ψ, Ψ	ψι *psee*
μ, Μ	μι *mee*		ω, Ω	ωμέγα *o-megha*

Streetwise

You should address a man as	κύριε	**kee**ree-e (Mr)
a married woman as	κυρία	kee**ree**-a (Mrs)
an unmarried woman or young woman as	δεσποινίς	dhespee**nees** (Miss)

Is it far/expensive?
Είναι μακριά;/Κοστίζει πολύ;
ee-ne makree-**a**/kos**tee**-zee po**lee**?

Are you ...?
Είσαι ...;
ee-se ...?

Do you understand?
Καταλαβαίνεις;
*kata-la-**ve**nees?*

Can you help me?
Μπορείτε να με βοηθήσετε;
*bo**ree**-te na me vo-ee**thee**-se-te?*

Where is the chemist's?
Πού είναι το φαρμακείο;
poo ee-ne to farma**kee**-o?

Where are the toilets?
Πού είναι οι τουαλέτες;
*poo **ee**-ne ee too-a-**le**-tes?*

How do I get there?
Πώς μπορώ να πάω εκεί;
*pos bo**ro** na pa-o e**kee**?*

What is this?
Τι είναι αυτό;
*tee **ee**-ne af**to**?*

How much is it?
Πόσο κάνει αυτό παρακαλώ;
*po*so *ka*nee af**to** para-ka**lo**?

How many kilometres?
Πόσα χιλιόμετρα;
*po*sa kheelee-**o**-metra?

Streetwise

At most beaches you are expected to pay for the use of changing rooms, deck chairs and showers. Such beaches normally have snack bars, a shop and a restaurant. Although nude bathing remains technically illegal, it is not uncommon in more secluded areas. Whether or not you are at risk of prosecution depends on the attitude of local authorities, so ask for local advice before you strip off!

Is it safe to swim here?	Μπορεί κανείς να κολυμπήσει εδώ άφοβα; *boree kanees na koleem-beesee edho afova*
How deep is the water?	Πόσο βαθειά είναι τα νερά; *poso vathee-a ee-ne ta nera?*
Are there strong currents?	Μήπως έχει δυνατά ρεύματα; *meepos ekhee dheena-ta rev-mata?*
Is it a private/quiet beach?	Είναι αυτή η παραλία ιδιωτική/ήσυχη; *ee-ne aftee ee paralee-a eedhee-oteekee/eesee-khee?*
Can I hire a deck chair/boat?	Μπορώ να νοικιάσω μία σαιζ-λονγκ/βάρκα; *boro na neekee-aso mee-a sez-long/varka?*
Can I go fishing/windsurfing?	Μπορώ να πάω για ψάρεμα/για γουίντ-σερφ; *boro na pa-o ya psa-rema/ya windsurf?*
Is there a children's pool?	Υπάρχει πισίνα για παιδιά; *eepar-khee pee-seena ya pedhee-a?*

See also **WATERSPORTS**

BREAKDOWNS

Streetwise

ELPA, the Automobile and Touring Club of Greece, offers free assistance to visitors who are members of motoring organisations in their own country. Dial 104 for their breakdown service. Those who are not members may be offered assistance if they join ELPA on the spot. You pay a subscription and a registration fee. For medical services, call 166.

My car has broken down	Το αυτοκίνητό μου έχει πάθει βλάβη *to afto-**kee**neeto moo ekhee **pa**thee **vla**vee*
There is something wrong with the brakes/the electrics	Κάτι δεν πάει καλά με τα φρένα/τα ηλεκτρονικά *katee dhen **pa**-ee ka**la** me ta **fre**na/ta eelek-tron**ee**ka*
There is a leak in the petrol tank/the radiator	Υπάρχει διαρροή στο ρεζερβουάρ βενζίνης/στο ψυγείο *ee**par**-khee dhee-aro-**ee** sto rezer**voo**ar ven**zee**nees/sto psee-**yee**-o*
The engine is overheating	Έχει υπερθερμανθεί η μηχανή *ekhee eeperthermanthee ee mee-khanee*
Can you tow me to a garage?	Μπορείτε να με ρυμουλκήσετε σ' ένα συνεργείο; *bo**ree**-te na me reemool-**kee**-se-te **se**na seener-**yee**-o?*
Can you send a mechanic/a breakdown van?	Μπορείτε να στείλετε έναν μηχανικό/ ένα κινητό συνεργείο; *bo**ree**-te na **stee**-le-te enan meekhan-ee**ko**/ena kee-nee**to** seener-**yee**-o?*
How long will it take to repair?	Σε πόσην ώρα θα είναι έτοιμο; *se **po**seen **o**ra tha **ee**-ne e**tee**mo?*

I have an appointment with ...	'Εχω ραντεβού με ... *ekho ran-de**voo** me ...*
Can I speak to Mr/Mrs ...?	**Μπορώ να μιλήσω στον Κύριο/στην Κυρία ...;** *bo**ro** na mee**lee**so ston **kee**reeo/steen kee**ree**a ...?*
He is expecting me	**Με περιμένει** *me peree-**me**nee*
Can I leave a message with his secretary?	**Μπορώ να αφήσω ένα μήνυμα με τη γραμματέα του;** *bo**ro** na a**fee**so **e**na **mee**neema me tee ghrama-**te**-a too?*
I am free tomorrow morning	**Είμαι ελεύθερος αύριο το πρωί** *ee-me el**ef**-theros **av**ree-o to pro-ee*
Can I send a telex from here?	**Μπορώ να στείλω ένα τέλεξ από δω;** *bo**ro** na **stee**lo **e**na telex a**po** dho?*
Where can I get some photocopying done?	**Πού μπορώ να βγάλω μερικές φωτοτυπίες;** *poo bo**ro** na **vgha**lo meree-**kes** foto-tee**pee**-es?*
I want to send this by courier	**Θέλω να το στείλω με συναποκόμιση** ***the**lo na to **stee**-lo me seenapoko**mee**see*
I will send you further details/a sample	**Θα σας στείλω περισσότερες λεπτομέρειες/ένα δείγμα** *tha sas **stee**lo peree-**so**-te-res lepto-**me**ree-es/**e**na **dhee**ghma*
Have you a catalogue/some literature ?	**'Εχετε έναν κατάλογο/πληροφορίες;** *ekh-e-te **e**nan ka**ta**-logho/pleero-fo**ree**-es?*

BUYING

Do you sell stamps?	**Πουλάτε γραμματόσημα;** *poolate ghrama-toseema?*
How much is that?	**Πόσο κάνει εκείνο εκεί;** *poso kanee ekee-no ekee?*
Have you anything smaller/bigger?	**Έχετε τίποτα μικρότερο/μεγαλύτερο;** *ekh-e-te tee-pota meekro-tero/megha-leetero?*
Have you got any bread/matches?	**Έχετε καθόλου ψωμί;/Έχετε σπίρτα;** *ekh-e-te kath-oloo psomee?/ekh-e-te speerta?*
I'd like some apples	**Θα ήθελα λίγα μήλα** *tha eethela leegha meela*
A packet of cigarettes, please	**Ένα κουτί τσιγάρα, παρακαλώ** *ena kootee tsee-ghara para-kalo*
I'll take this one/ that one there	**Θα ήθελα αυτό εδώ/εκείνο εκεί** *tha eethela afto edho/ekee-no ekee*
I think you've given me the wrong change	**Νομίζω πως μου έχετε δώσει λάθος ρέστα** *nomeezo pos moo ekhe-te dhosee lathos resta*

See also **MEASUREMENTS, PAYING, SHOPPING**

Streetwise

Camping is only permitted on official sites. If you can't find a site, contact the Tourist Police.

We are looking for a camp site	Ψάχνουμε για κάποιο κάμπιγκ *psakh-noo-me ya kapee-o camping*
Do you have any vacancies?	Έχετε θέσεις; *ekhe-te thesees?*
How much is it per night?	Πόσο κοστίζει η διανυχτέρευση; *poso kostee-zee ee dhee-aneekh-terevsee?*
We want to stay one night	Θέλουμε να μείνουμε για μία νύχτα *theloo-me na meenoo-me ya mee-a neekh-ta*
May we camp here?	Μπορούμε να κατασκηνώσουμε εδώ; *boroo-me na kata-skeeno-soo-me edho?*
Can we park our caravan there?	Μπορούμε να παρκάρουμε το τροχόσπιτό μας εδώ; *boroo-me na parka-roo-me to trokho-speeto mas edho?*
What facilities do you have on the site?	Τι ανέσεις έχετε στο κάμπιγκ; *tee a-nesees ekhe-te sto camping?*
Is there electricity?	Υπάρχει ηλεκτρικό ρεύμα; *eepar-khee eelek-treeko revma?*

CAR HIRE

Streetwise

Car hire is expensive compared with other European countries. To hire a car you must be over 21 years of age and have held a full licence for at least a year. Taxes and duties may be added so make sure you know on what basis you will be charged.

I want to hire a car	Θέλω να νοικιάσω ένα αυτοκίνητο *thelo na neekee-aso ena afto-keeneeto*
I need a car with a chauffeur	Χρειάζομαι αυτοκίνητο με σωφέρ *khree-azo-me afto-keeneeto me sofer*
I want a large/small car	Θέλω ένα μεγάλο/μικρό αυτοκίνητο *thelo ena meghalo/meekro afto-keeneeto*
Is there a charge per kilometre?	Υπάρχει τιμή ανά χιλιόμετρο; *eepar-khee teemee ana kheelee-ometro?*
How much extra is the comprehensive insurance cover?	Πόσο επιπλέον κοστίζει μία πλήρης ασφαλιστική κάλυψη; *poso epee-ple-on kostee-zee mee-a pleerees asfalee-steekee kaleepsee?*
I would like to leave the car in ...	Θα ήθελα να αφήσω το αυτοκίνητο ... *tha ee-thela na a-feeso to afto-keeneeto ...*
My husband/wife will be driving as well	Ο/Η σύζυγός μου θα οδηγεί επίσης *o/ee seezee-ghos moo tha odhee-yee epee-sees*
Is there a radio/radio-cassette?	Υπάρχει ραδιόφωνο/ραδιοκασετόφωνο; *eepar-khee radhee-ofono/radhee-okase-tofono?*
How do I operate the controls?	Πώς λειτουργούν αυτά τα κουμπιά; *pos leetoor-ghoon afta ta koombee-a?*

CHEMIST'S

Streetwise

Chemists operate a rota system whereby at least one chemist's
(ΦΑΡΜΑΚΕΙΟΝ – pharma**kee**-on) is open outside normal hours. A list
of chemists' open at night and on Sundays is displayed on the door of
all chemists'.

I want something for a headache/a sore throat/ toothache	Θέλω κάτι για τον πονοκέφαλο/για πονόλαιμο/για τον πονόδοντο *thelo katee ya ton pono-kefalo/ya pono-lemo/ ya ton pono-dhondo*
I would like some aspirin/sticking plaster	Θα ήθελα μία ασπιρίνη/ένα λευκοπλάστη *tha eethela mee-a aspee-reenee/ena lefkoplastee*
Have you anything for insect bites/ sunburn/diarrhoea?	Έχετε κάτι για τσιμπήματα εντόμων/εγκαύματα ηλίου/διάρροια; *ekhe-te katee ya tsimbee-mata endomon/ engav-mata eelee-oo/dhee-aree-a?*
I have a cold/a cough	Έχω κρυολογήσει/βήχα *ekho kreeolo-yeesee/veekha*
Is this suitable for an upset stomach/hay fever?	Είναι αυτό κατάλληλο για διαταραγμένο στομάχι/αλλεργικό συνάχι; *ee-ne afto kata-leelo ya dhee-ataragh-meno stoma-khee/alleryeeko seenakhee?*
How much/How many do I take?	Πόσο/Πόσα πρέπει να παίρνω; *poso/posa prepee na perno?*
Is it safe for children?	Είναι άφοβο για παιδιά; *eene afovo ya pedhee-a?*

CHILDREN

Streetwise

Children are normally well catered for in Greece and are welcome everywhere including bars and restaurants. There are many reductions for children available on transport, in hotels, etc. Check with the local tourist office for details.

I have two children	Έχω δύο παιδιά *ekho **dhee**-o pedhee-**a***
Do you have a special rate for children?	Έχετε μειωμένες τιμές για παιδιά; *ekhe-te mee-**omenes** tee**mes** ya pedhee-**a**?*
Do you have facilities for children?	Έχετε ευκολίες για παιδιά; *ekhe-te efko**lee**es ya pedhee-**a**?*
Have you got a cot for the baby?	Έχετε κρεβατάκι για το μωρό; *ekhe-te kreva**takee** ya to mo**ro**?*
Do you have a special menu for children?	Έχετε ειδικό μενού για παιδιά; *ekhe-te eedhee-**ko** me**noo** ya pedhee-**a**?*
Where can I feed/change the baby?	Πού μπορώ να ταΐσω/αλλάξω το μωρό; *poo bo**ro** na ta-**eeso**/a**lakso** to mo**ro**?*
Where can I warm the baby's bottle?	Πού μπορώ να ζεστάνω το μπιμπερό του μωρού; *poo bo**ro** na zes**tano** to bee-be**ro** too mo**roo**?*
Is there a baby-sitting service?	Υπάρχει υπηρεσία μπέυμπυ-σίττινγκ; *ee**par**-khee eepeere**seea** babysitting?*

CHURCH & WORSHIP

Streetwise

The predominant church in Greece is the Greek Orthodox Church. Protestant and Roman Catholic churches are also to be found in Athens and other large towns. Churches are on the whole open for most of the day and early evening. To gain entry to a church which is closed, ask for the key, which is normally held at the nearest household or at the local café. In most parts of Greece and especially on the islands, when visiting a church men should wear long trousers and women be suitably covered (but not by wearing trousers).

Where is the nearest church?	Πού είναι η πιο κοντινή εκκλησία; *poo **ee**-ne ee pee-o kondee-**nee** ekleesee-a?*
Where is there a Protestant/Catholic church?	Πού υπάρχει εκκλησία διαμαρτυρομένων/ καθολικών; *poo ee**par**-khee ekleesee-a dhee-amarteero**me**non/katholee**kon**?*
I want to see a priest	Θέλω να δω έναν ιερέα ***the**lo na dho **e**nan ee-e**re**-a*
What time is the service?	Τι ώρα είναι η λειτουργία; *tee **o**ra **ee**-ne ee leetoor-**yee**-a?*
I want to go to confession	Θέλω να πάω στην εξομολόγηση ***the**lo na **pa**-o steen ekso-mo**lo**-yeesee*
Is it possible to visit the church?	Είναι δυνατό να επισκεφθώ την εκκλησία; ***ee**-ne dheena**to** na episkef**tho** teen ekkleesee-a?*

CITY TRAVEL

When travelling on city buses you should have the exact fare ready before you get onto the bus. You then drop the money into the box by the driver as you get on.

Does this bus/train go to ...?

Πηγαίνει αυτό το λεωφορείο/τραίνο ...;
pee-yenee afto to leo-foree-o/treno ...?

Which number bus goes to ...?

Ποιο λεωφορείο πηγαίνει ...;
peeo leo-foree-o pee-yenee ...?

Where do I get a bus for the airport/the cathedral?

Από πού παίρνω το λεωφορείο για το αεροδρόμιο/για τη μητρόπολη;
apo poo perno to leo-foree-o ya to aero-dhromee-o/ya tee meetro-polee?

Where is the nearest underground station?

Πού είναι ο κοντινότερος σταθμός υπογείου;
poo ee-ne o kondee-no-teros stath-mos eepo-yee-oo?

What is the fare to the town centre?

Πόσο είναι το εισιτήριο για το κέντρο της πόλης;
poso ee-ne to eesee-teeree-o ya to kendro tees polees?

Where do I buy a ticket?

Από πού αγοράζω εισιτήριο;
apo poo agho-razo eesee-teeree-o?

What time is the last bus?

Τι ώρα είναι το τελευταίο λεωφορείο;
tee ora ee-ne to telef-te-o leo-foree-o?

Streetwise

There are very few laundrettes in Greece. Use your hotel laundry service if there is one – these services are normally fairly efficient.

Is there a laundry service?	Έχετε υπηρεσία πλυντηρίου; *ekhe-te eepeereseea pleendeereeoo?*
Is there a laundrette/dry-cleaner's nearby?	Υπάρχει κανένα πλυντήριο/καθαριστήριο εδώ κοντά; *eepar-khee ka-nena pleen-deeree-o/katharee-steeree-o edho konda?*
Where can I get this skirt cleaned/ironed?	Πού μπορούν να μου καθαρίσουν/σιδερώσουν αυτή τη φούστα; *poo boroon na moo katha-reesoon/seedhee-rosoon aftee tee foosta?*
Where can I do some washing?	Πού μπορώ να πλύνω μερικά ρούχα; *poo boro na pleeno meree-ka rookha?*
Where can I dry my clothes?	Πού μπορώ να στεγνώσω τα ρούχα μου; *poo boro na stegh-noso ta rookha moo?*
The stain is coffee/blood	Ο λεκές είναι από καφέ/αίμα *o le-kes eene apo ka-fe/ema*
When will my things be ready?	Πότε θα είναι έτοιμα τα ρούχα μου; *po-te tha ee-ne etee-ma ta rookha moo?*

CLOTHES

I take a size …

Φοράω το νούμερο …
*fora-o to **noo**-mero …*

Can you measure me please?

Μπορείτε να μου πάρετε τα μέτρα, παρακαλώ;
*bo**ree**-te na moo **pa**-re-te ta **me**tra, para-ka**lo**?*

May I try on this dress?

Μπορώ να δοκιμάσω αυτό το φόρεμα;
*bo**ro** na dhokee-**ma**so a**fto** to **fo**-rema?*

May I take it over to the light?

Μπορώ να το δω στο φως;
*bo**ro** na to dho sto fos?*

Where are the changing rooms?

Πού είναι τα αποδυτήρια;
*poo **ee**-ne ta apodhee-**tee**ree-a?*

Is there a mirror?

Πού υπάρχει καθρέφτης;
*poo ee**par**-khee kath-**ref**tees?*

It's too big/small

Είναι πολύ μεγάλο/μικρό
ee**-ne po**lee** megh-**a**lo/mee**kro

What is the material?

Τι είναι το υλικό;
*tee **ee**-ne to eelee-**ko**?*

Is it washable?

Πλένεται;
***ple**-ne-te?*

I don't like it

Δεν μου αρέσει
*dhen moo a-**re**see*

I don't like the colour

Δεν μου αρέσει το χρώμα
*dhen moo a-**re**see to **khro**ma*

COACH TRAVEL

Streetwise

There are two main coach operators in Greece: OSE is the state railway service, and it operates coaches from many mainline railway stations. KTEL is a consortium of private companies. It has its own bus stations in many Greek towns and cities.

Is there a bus to …?	Έχει λεωφορείο για …; *ekhee leo-foree-o ya …?*
Where do I catch the bus for …?	Από πού παίρνω το λεωφορείο για …; *apo poo perno to leo-foree-o ya …?*
What are the times of the buses to …?	Τι ώρες έχει λεωφορείο για …; *tee o-res ekhee leo-foree-o ya …?*
Does this bus go to …?	Πηγαίνει αυτό το λεωφορείο για …; *pee-yenee afto to leo-foree-o ya …?*
Where do I get off?	Πού κατεβαίνω; *poo ka-te-veno?*
What time does it leave?	Τι ώρα φεύγει; *tee ora fev-yee?*
What time does it arrive?	Τι ώρα φτάνει; *tee ora ftanee?*
Will you tell me where to get off?	Μου λέτε πού να κατέβω; *moo le-te poo na katevo?*
Let me off here, please	Κατεβάστε με εδώ, παρακαλώ *ka-te-vaste me edho para-kalo*
Where is the bus station?	Πού είναι ο σταθμός των λεωφορείων; *Poo ee-ne o stathmos ton leoforeeon?*

COMPLAINTS

| This does not work | Αυτό εδώ δεν λειτουργεί |
| | *afto edho dhen leetoor-yee* |

| I can't turn the heating off/on | Δεν μπορώ να κλείσω/ανοίξω το καλοριφέρ |
| | *dhen boro na kleeso/aneekso to kalo-reefer* |

| The lock is broken | Έχει σπάσει η κλειδαριά |
| | *ekhee spasee ee klee-dharee-a* |

| I can't open the window | Δεν μπορώ να ανοίξω το παράθυρο |
| | *dhen boro na aneekso to para-theero* |

| The toilet won't flush | Το καζανάκι δεν τρέχει |
| | *to kaza-nakee dhen trekhee* |

| There is no hot water/ toilet paper | Δεν υπάρχει ζεστό νερό/χαρτί τουαλέτας |
| | *dhen eepar-khee zesto nero/khartee too-aletas* |

| The washbasin is dirty | Ο νιπτήρας είναι λερωμένος |
| | *o neep-teeras ee-ne lero-menos* |

| The room is noisy | Το δωμάτιο έχει φασαρία |
| | *to dhomatee-o ekhee fasaree-a* |

| We are still waiting to be served | Περιμένουμε τόση ώρα για να παραγγείλουμε |
| | *peree-menoo-me tosee ora ya na paran-geeloo-me* |

| I bought this here yesterday | Αγόρασα αυτό από δω, χθες |
| | *agho-rasa afto apo dho khthes* |

| It has a flaw/hole in it | Έχει κάποιο ελάττωμα/μία τρύπα |
| | *ekhee kapee-o ela-toma/mee-a treepa* |

Streetwise

It is customary to shake hands on both meeting and parting. Kissing, however, is restricted to family and close friends.

How do you do?	Χαίρω πολύ *khero polee*
Hello/Goodbye	Γεια σας/Γεια σας *ya sas/ya sas*
Do you speak English?	Μιλάτε Αγγλικά; *meela-te anglee-ka?*
I don't speak Greek	Δεν μιλάω Ελληνικά *dhen meela-o elee-neeka*
What's your name?	Πώς σε λένε; *pos se le-ne?*
My name is ...	Με λένε ... *me le-ne ...*
Do you mind if I sit here?	Σας πειράζει αν καθήσω εδώ; *sas peera-zee an kathee-so edho?*
I'm English/Scottish/Welsh	Είμαι Εγγλέζος/Σκωτσέζος/Ουαλός *ee-me en-glezos/skot-sezos/oo-alos*
Are you Greek?	Είσαστε Έλληνας; *eesa-ste elee-nas?*
Would you like to come out with me?	Θα θέλατε να βγούμε έξω μαζί; *tha thela-te na vghoo-me ekso mazee?*
Yes, I should like to	Ναι, θα μου άρεσε κάτι τέτοιο *ne, tha moo a-re-se katee tetee-o*

No, thank you	Όχι, ευχαριστώ
	okhee ef-kharee-sto
Yes, please	Ναι, παρακαλώ
	ne parakalo
Thank you (very much)	Ευχαριστώ (πολύ)
	ef-kharee-sto (polee)
Don't mention it	Παρακαλώ
	para-kalo
I'm sorry	Με συγχωρείτε
	me seen-khoree-te
I'm on holiday here	Βρίσκομαι εδώ για διακοπές
	vreesko-me edho ya dhee-akopes
Do you mind if I smoke?	Σας πειράζει να καπνίσω;
	sas peera-zee na kap-neeso?
Would you like a drink?	Θέλετε ένα ποτό;
	the-le-te ena poto?
Have you ever been to Britain?	Έχετε ποτέ πάει στη Βρετανία;
	ekhe-te po-te pa-ee stee vretanee-a?
Did you like it there?	Σας άρεσε εκεί;
	sas a-re-se ekee?
What part of Greece are you from?	Από ποιο μέρος της Ελλάδας είσαστε;
	apo pee-o meros tees ela-dhas eesa-ste?

CONVERSION CHARTS

In the weight and length charts the middle figure can be either metric or imperial. Thus 3.3 feet = 1 metre, 1 foot = 0.3 metres, and so on.

feet		metres	inches		cm	lbs		kg
3.3	1	0.3	0.39	1	2.54	2.2	1	0.45
6.6	2	0.61	0.79	2	5.08	4.4	2	0.91
9.9	3	0.91	1.18	3	7.62	6.6	3	1.4
13.1	4	1.22	1.57	4	10.6	8.8	4	1.8
16.4	5	1.52	1.97	5	12.7	11	5	2.2
19.7	6	1.83	2.36	6	15.2	13.2	6	2.7
23	7	2.13	2.76	7	17.8	15.4	7	3.2
26.2	8	2.44	3.15	8	20.3	17.6	8	3.6
29.5	9	2.74	3.54	9	22.9	19.8	9	4.1
32.9	10	3.05	3.9	10	25.4	22	10	4.5
			4.3	11	27.9			
			4.7	12	30.1			

°C	0	5	10	15	17	20	22	24	26	28	30	35	37	38	40	50	100
°F	32	41	50	59	63	68	72	75	79	82	86	95	98.4	100	104	122	212

Km	10	20	30	40	50	60	70	80	90	100	110	120
Miles	6.2	12.4	18.6	24.9	31	37.3	43.5	49.7	56	62	68.3	74.6

Tyre pressures

lb/sq in	15	18	20	22	24	26	28	30	33	35
kg/sq cm	1.1	1.3	1.4	1.5	1.7	1.8	2	2.1	2.3	2.5

Liquids

gallons	1.1	2.2	3.3	4.4	5.5
litres	5	10	15	20	25

pints	0.44	0.88	1.76
litres	0.25	0.5	1

I have nothing to declare	Δεν έχω να δηλώσω τίποτα *dhen ekho na dhee-loso tee-pota*
I have the usual allowances of alchohol/tobacco	Έχω ότι επιτρέπει ο κανονισμός για οινοπνευματώδη/καπνό *ekho otee epee-trepee o kanoneesmos ya eenopnevma-todhee/kapno*
I have two bottles of wine/a bottle of spirits to declare	Έχω να δηλώσω δύο μπουκάλια κρασί/ ένα μπουκάλι με οινοπνευματώδες ποτό *ekho na dhee-loso dhee-o bookalee-a krasee/ ena boo-kalee me eenop-nevma-todhes poto*
My wife/husband and I have a joint passport	Η/Ο σύζυγός μου και εγώ έχουμε οικογενειακό διαβατήριο *ee/o seezee-ghos moo ke egho ekhoo-me eeko-yenee-ako dhee-ava-teeree-o*
The children are on this passport	Τα παιδιά είναι σ' αυτό το διαβατήριο *ta pedhee-a ee-ne safto to dhee-ava-teeree-o*
I am a British national	Είμαι Βρετανός υπήκοος *ee-me vreta-nos eepeeko-os*
I shall be staying in this country for three weeks	Θα μείνω στη χώρα σας για τρεις εβδομάδες *tha meeno stee khora sas ya trees ev-dho-madhes*
We are on holiday	Είμαστε εδώ για διακοπές *eema-ste edho ya dhee-ako-pes*
I am here on business	Είμαι εδώ για δουλειές *eeme edho ya dhoolee-es*
I have an entry visa	Έχω βίζα *ekho veeza*

What is the date today?	Τι ημερομηνία είναι σήμερα;	*tee eemero-mee**nee**-a **ee**-ne **see**mera?*
It's the … 2nd of June	Είναι … δύο Ιουνίου	*ee-ne …* *dhee-o eeoonee-oo*
We will arrive on the 29th of August	Θα φτάσουμε στις είκοσι εννέα Αυγούστου	*tha **ft**asoo-me stees **ee**-kosee ene-a av-**ghoo**stoo*
1984	χίλια εννιακόσα ογδόντα τέσσερα	*khee**lee**-a enee-a**ko**sa ogh-**dhon**da **te**sera*
Monday	Δευτέρα	*dhef-**te**ra*
Tuesday	Τρίτη	***tree**tee*
Wednesday	Τετάρτη	*te-**tar**tee*
Thursday	Πέμπτη	***pemb**-tee*
Friday	Παρασκευή	*para-ske**vee***
Saturday	Σάββατο	***sa**vato*
Sunday	Κυριακή	*keeree-a**kee***
January	Ιανουάριος	*eeanoo-**aree**-os*
February	Φεβρουάριος	*fevroo-**aree**-os*
March	Μάρτιος	***mar**tee-os*
April	Απρίλιος	*a**pree**lee-os*
May	Μάιος	***ma**-ee-os*
June	Ιούνιος	*ee**oo**nee-os*
July	Ιούλιος	*ee**oo**lee-os*
August	Αύγουστος	***av**-ghoostos*
September	Σεπτέμβριος	*sep**tem**-vree-os*
October	Οκτώβριος	*ok**to**vree-os*
November	Νοέμβριος	*no-**em**vree-os*
December	Δεκέμβριος	*dhe**kem**-vree-os*

DENTIST

Streetwise

Form E111, which you should obtain from the DSS before you leave the UK, entitles you to free medical treatment in Greece. However, the general standard of state dentists is not particularly high, so it is worth taking out an insurance policy to cover any private treatment you may require.

I need to see the dentist (urgently)	Πρέπει να δω τον οδοντογιατρό (επειγόντως) **pre**pee na dho ton odhondo-ya**tro** (epee-**ghon**dos)
I have toothache	Έχω πονόδοντο ekho po**no**-dhondo
I've broken a tooth	Έσπασα ένα δόντι **e**spasa ena dhondee
A filling has come out	Μου έχει ξεκολλήσει ένα σφράγισμα moo **e**khee kse-ko**lee**see ena **sfra**-yeesma
My gums are bleeding/are sore	Έχω ματωμένα ούλα/Τα ούλα μου με πονάνε ekho mato-**me**na **oo**la/ta **oo**la moo me po**na**-ne
Please give me an injection	Παρακαλώ, κάντε μου μία ένεση para-ka**lo** kande moo **mee**-a e-nesee

THE DENTIST MAY SAY:

Θα πρέπει να σας το βγάλω tha **pre**pee na sas to **vgha**lo	I shall have to take it out
Χρειάζεστε σφράγισμα khree-**a**-zes-te **sfra**-yeesma	You need a filling
Ίσως σας πονέσει λιγάκι **ee**sos sas po-**ne**see lee**gha**-kee	This might hurt a bit

Streetwise

To attract someone's attention, you should say συγγνώμη, *seegnomee, (excuse me).*

Excuse me, where is the nearest post office?	Συγγνώμη, πού είναι το πιο κοντινό ταχυδρομείο; *seegnomee poo **ee**-ne to pee-o kondee-**no** takhee-dhro**mee**-o?*
How do I get to the airport?	Πώς μπορώ να πάω στο αεροδρόμιο; *pos boro na **pa**-o sto aero-**dhro**mee-o?*
Is this the right way to the cathedral?	Είναι αυτός ο δρόμος για την μητρόπολη; *ee-ne aftos o **dhro**mos ya teen mee**tro**-polee?*
Is it far to walk/ by car?	Είναι μακριά με τα πόδια/το αυτοκίνητο; *ee-ne makree-**a** me ta **po**dhee-a/to afto-**kee**neeto?*
Which road do I take for ...?	Ποιον δρόμο πρέπει να πάρω για ...; *pee-on **dhro**mo **pre**pee na **pa**ro ya ...?*
I am looking for the tourist information office	Ψάχνω τις τουριστικές πληροφορίες ***psakh**-no tees tooree-stee**kes** pleero-fo**ree**-es*
Is this the turning for ...?	Από δω πρέπει να στρίψω για ...; *apo dho **pre**pee na streep-so ya ...?*
I have lost my way	Έχω χαθεί *ekho kha**thee***

DOCTOR

Streetwise

Form E111, which you should obtain from the DSS before you leave the UK, entitles you to free medical treatment in Greece. However, the general standards of state hospitals and state doctors may not be up to what you are used to, so it is worth taking out an insurance policy to cover private medical treatment and the costs of repatriation in the event of serious illness or injury.

I need a doctor	Χρειάζομαι γιατρό khree-*azome* ya*tro*
Can I have an appointment?	Μου κλείνετε ραντεβού; moo **klee**-ne-te ran-de**voo**?
My son/wife is ill	Ο γιος μου είναι άρρωστος/η γυναίκα μου είναι άρρωστη o yos moo **ee**-ne arostos/ee yee-**ne**ka moo **ee**ne **a**rostee
I have a sore throat/ a stomach upset	Έχω πονόλαιμο/στομαχική διαταραχή ekho pono-lemo/stoma-khee**kee** dhe-atara-**khee**
He has diarrhoea/ earache	Έχει διάρροια/Τον πονάει το αυτί του ekhee dhe-aree-a/ton po*na*-ee to af**tee** too
I have a pain in my chest/here	Πονάω στο στήθος/εδώ po*na*-o sto **stee**thos/e*dho*
He has been stung/ bitten	Τον τσίμπησε/δάγκωσε ton **tseem**bee-se/**dhan**go-se
He can't breathe/ walk	Δεν μπορεί να αναπνεύσει/περπατήσει dhen bo*ree* na anap**nev**-see/perpa**tee**see

| I feel dizzy | Έχω ζαλάδα |
| | *ekho zaladha* |

| I can't sleep/ swallow | Έχω αϋπνίες/Δεν μπορώ να καταπιώ |
| | *ekho a-eepnee-es/dhen boro na katapee-o* |

| She has been sick | Έκανε εμετό |
| | *eka-ne emeto* |

| I am diabetic/ pregnant | Είμαι διαβητικός/έγκυος |
| | *ee-me dhee-avee-teekos/engee-os* |

| I am allergic to … | Είμαι αλλεργικός σε… |
| | *ee-me aleryeekos se …* |

| I have high blood pressure | Είμαι υπερτασικός |
| | *ee-me eeper-taseekos* |

| My blood group is A positive | Είμαι ομάδα αίματος Α θετικό |
| | *ee-me omadha ematos alfa thetee-ko* |

THE DOCTOR MAY SAY:

Πρέπει να μείνετε στο κρεβάτι
prepee na meene-te sto kreva-tee

You must stay in bed

Θα πρέπει να πάει στο νοσοκομείο
tha prepee na pa-ee sto noso-komee-o

He will have to go to hospital

Θα χρειαστείτε εγχείρηση
tha khree-astee-te enkhee-reesee

You will need an operation

33

DRINKS

Streetwise

*Greek coffee – (ελληνικός καφές elleenee-**kos** ka**fes**) is served, black and very strong, in small cups. You can ask for it without sugar (σκέτος **ske**-tos), with sugar (μέτριος **metrios**), or sweet (γλυκύς ghlee-**kees**). It normally comes with a glass of water (νερό ne**ro**). Instant coffee (known by the brand name Nescafé) is popular and you may ask for it with milk (με γάλα me **gha**la) or as iced coffee (φραπέ fra**pe**). Tea (τσάι **tsa**-ee) is served with milk or with lemon (λεμόνι le**mo**nee).*

A black coffee/A white coffee, please	Ένα καφέ/Ένα καφέ με γάλα παρακαλώ *ena ka**fe**/ena ka**fe** me **gha**la para-ka**lo***
Two cups of tea	Δύο φλυτζάνια τσάι *dhee-o fleedzanee-a **tsa**-ee*
A pot of tea for four	Τσάι για τέσσερις *tsa-ee ya **te**-serees*
A glass of lemonade	Μία λεμονάδα *mee-a lemo-**nadha***
A bottle of mineral water	Ένα μπουκάλι επιτραπέζιο νερό *ena boo-**kalee** epeetra**pe**zeeo ne**ro***
Do you have ...?	Έχετε ...; *ekhe-te ...?*
Another coffee, please	Ένα καφέ ακόμα παρακαλώ *ena ka-**fe** a**ko**ma para-ka**lo***
With milk/ice	Με γάλα/παγάκια *me **gha**la/pagha**kee**-a*

See also **WINES & SPIRITS**

Streetwise

Remember to keep to the right-hand side of the road and overtake on the left, and that traffic from the right has priority unless otherwise indicated. The speed limit is 50km/h in towns and 100km/h on the highways. Seat belts are compulsory for both the driver and the front seat passenger. Special care should be taken when traversing unguarded level crossings.

Is there a toll on this motorway?	**Υπάρχουν διόδια σ' αυτόν τον αυτοκινητόδρομο;** *ee**par**-khoon dhee-**odh**ee-a saf**ton** ton afto-keenee-**to**dhromo?*
What is causing this hold-up?	**Σε τι οφείλεται αυτή η συμφόρηση;** *se tee o**fee**-le-te af**tee** ee seem**fo**-reesee?*
Is there a short cut?	**Υπάρχει παράκαμψη;** *ee**par**-khee para**kamp**-see?*
Where can I park?	**Πού μπορώ να παρκάρω;** *poo bo**ro** na par**ka**ro?*
Is there a car park nearby?	**Υπάρχει πάρκινγκ εδώ κοντά;** *ee**par**-khee parking **edho** kon**da**?*
Can I park here?	**Μπορώ να παρκάρω εδώ;** *bo**ro** na par**ka**ro **edho**?*
How long can I stay here?	**Πόσο μπορώ να μείνω εδώ;** **po**so bo**ro** na **mee**no **edho**?

See also **ACCIDENTS – CARS, BREAKDOWNS, PETROL STATION, POLICE**

EATING OUT

Streetwise

Tavernas are less formal than restaurants and are more likely to serve traditional Greek fare. They may not have a proper menu and you may even find yourself being invited into the kitchen to choose what you want to eat. Fixed-price meals are more likely to be found in restaurants.

Is there a restaurant/
café near here?

Υπάρχει εστιατόριο/καφενείο εδώ κοντά;
eepar-khee estee-atoree-o/kafenee-o edho konda?

A table for four,
please

'Ενα τραπέζι για τέσσερις, παρακαλώ
ena trapezee ya te-serees para-kalo

May we see the
menu?

Μπορούμε να δούμε το μενού;
boroo-me na dhoo-me to menoo?

We'd like a drink
first

Θα θέλαμε κάτι να πιούμε πρώτα
tha thela-me katee na pee-oo-me prota

Do you have a menu
for children?

'Εχετε ειδικό μενού για παιδιά;
ekhe-te eedhee-ko menoo ya pedhee-a ?

We'd like a dessert/
some mineral water

Θα θέλαμε επιδόρπιο/λίγο επιτραπέζιο
νερό
tha thela-me epee-dhorpee-o/leegho epeetrapezee-o nero

The bill, please

Το λογαριασμό παρακαλώ
to logharee-asmo para-kalo

Is service included?

Συμπεριλαμβάνεται και το φιλοδώρημα;
seem-beree-lamva-ne-te ke to feelodhoreema?

See also **DRINKS, MENUS, ORDERING, PAYING**

Streetwise

Emergency telephone numbers:

First Aid	166
Police	100
Fire Brigade	199
ELPA (Automobile and Touring Club of Greece)	104
Tourist Police	171

There's a fire!	**Φωτιά!** *fotee-a!*
Call a doctor/an ambulance	**Καλέστε ένα γιατρό/ασθενοφόρο** *ka-le-ste ena yatro/astheno-foro*
We must get him to hospital	**Πρέπει να τον πάμε στο νοσοκομείο** *prepee na ton pa-me sto noso-komee-o*
Fetch help quickly	**Φέρτε βοήθεια γρήγορα** *fer-te vo-eethee-a ghree-ghora*
He can't swim	**Δεν ξέρει κολύμπι** *dhen kseree koleem-bee*
Where's the nearest police station?	**Πού είναι το πιο κοντινό αστυνομικό τμήμα;** *poo ee-ne to pee-o kondee-no asteeno-meeko tmee-ma?*
My child/My handbag is missing	**Έχασα το παιδί μου/την τσάντα μου** *ekhasa to pedhee moo/teen tsan-da moo*
My watch has been stolen	**Μου έκλεψαν το ρολόι** *moo eklep-san to rolo-ee*
I've forgotten my key	**Έχω ξεχάσει το κλειδί μου** *ekho kse-khasee to klee-dhee moo*

See also **ACCIDENTS, BREAKDOWNS, DENTIST, DOCTOR**

ENTERTAINMENT

Streetwise

Open-air cinemas are in use in the summer. Film soundtracks are normally in the original language.

Are there any local festivals?	Γίνονται τίποτα τοπικές γιορτές; *yeenon-de **tee**-pota topee-**kes** yor-**tes**?*
Can you recommend something for the children?	Έχετε να μου συστήσετε κάτι για τα παιδιά; *ekhe-te na moo sees**tee**-se-te **ka**tee ya ta pedhee-**a**?*
What is there to do in the evenings?	Πού μπορούμε να πηγαίνουμε τα βράδια; *poo bo**roo**-me na pee-**ye**noo-me ta **vra**dhee-a?*
Where is there a cinema/theatre?	Πού υπάρχει σινεμά/θέατρο; *poo ee**par**-khee see-ne**ma**/**the**-atro?*
Are there any nightclubs/discos?	Υπάρχουν εδώ νάιτ-κλαμπ/δισκοθήκες; *ee**par**-khoon e**dho** nightclub/dheesko**thee**kes?*
Can you book the tickets for us?	Μπορείτε να μας κρατήσετε εισιτήρια; *bo**ree**-te na mas kra**tee**-se-te eesee-**tee**ree-a?*
Is there a swimming pool?	Υπάρχει καμιά πισίνα εδώ κοντά; *ee**par**-khee kamee-**a** pee-**see**na e**dho** kon**da**?*

See also **NIGHTLIFE, SIGHTSEEING**

Streetwise

A list of ferry schedules is available from the Greek Tourist Office in London. Otherwise up-to-date information may be sought from the Port Police in Piraeus and other ports. Tickets may be bought on board ferries but if you are travelling by car make sure you book in advance, especially in high season.

What time is the next sailing?	Τι ώρα είναι το επόμενο φέρρυ; *tee ora ee-ne to epo-meno feree?*
A return ticket for one car and two passengers	Εισιτήριο με επιστροφή για ένα αυτοκίνητο και δύο άτομα *eesee-teeree-o me epee-strofee ya ena afto-keeneeto ke dhee-o atoma*
How long does the crossing take?	Πόσην ώρα για να πάμε απέναντι; *poseen ora ya na pa-me ape-nandee?*
Are there any cabins/reclining seats?	Υπάρχουν καμπίνες/ανακλινόμενα καθίσματα; *eepar-khoon kabee-nes/anaklee-no-mena kathees-mata?*
Is there a TV lounge/bar?	Υπάρχει αίθουσα τηλεόρασης/μπαρ; *eepar-khee ethoo-sa teele-orasees/bar?*
Where are the toilets?	Πού είναι οι τουαλέτες; *poo ee-ne ee too-aletes?*
Can we go out on deck?	Μπορούμε να βγούμε στο κατάστρωμα; *boroo-me na vghoo-me sto kata-stroma?*
What is the sea like today?	Πώς είναι η θάλασσα σήμερα; *pos ee-ne ee thala-sa see-mera?*

GIFTS & SOUVENIRS

Where can we buy souvenirs of the cathedral?	Πού μπορούμε να αγοράσουμε ενθύμια του ναού; *poo boroo-me na aghora-soo-me entheemee-a too na-oo?*
I want to buy a present for my husband/my wife	Θέλω να αγοράσω ένα δώρο για τον άνδρα μου/τη γυναίκα μου *thelo na agho-raso ena dhoro ya ton andhra moo/tee yee-neka moo*
What is the local speciality?	Τι φτιάχνουν εδώ; *tee ftee-akhnoon edho?*
Is this hand-made?	Είναι χειροποίητο; *ee-ne kheeropee-eeto?*
Have you anything suitable for a young child?	Έχετε τίποτα κατάλληλο για ένα μικρό παιδί; *ekhe-te teepota kata-leelo ya ena meekro pedhee?*
I want something cheaper/more expensive	Θέλω κάτι πιο φτηνό/ακριβό *thelo katee pee-o fteeno/akree-vo*
Please wrap it up for me	Μου το τυλίγετε σας παρακαλώ *moo to teelee-ye-te sas para-kalo*

The following basic rules of Greek grammar will help you make full use of the information in this book.

Nouns

Greek nouns can be *masculine, feminine* or *neuter*, and the words for 'the' and 'a' (the articles) change according to the gender of the noun:

ένας = 'a' *with masc. nouns*
μία = 'a' *with fem. nouns*
ένα = 'a' *with neuter nouns*

ο (οι) = 'the' *with masc. (plural) nouns*
η (οι) = 'the' *with fem. (plural) nouns*
το (τα) = 'the' *with neuter (plural) nouns*

The article is the most reliable indication of the gender of a noun. In the dictionary sections you will come across examples like this: 'ο/η γιατρός doctor'. This means that the same ending is used for male as for female doctors, i.e. ο γιατρός is a male doctor, while η γιατρός is a female doctor.

You will also encounter entries like ο Άγγλος/η Αγγλίδα; indicating that an Englishman is referred to as ο Άγγλος while the (ending of the) noun changes to η Αγγλίδα when applied to a woman.

The most common endings of *masculine* nouns are: **-ος, -ας, -ης**, e.g:

ο άνδρας   man
ο πατέρας   father
ο κυβερνήτης   captain *(of aeroplane)*

The most common endings of *feminine* nouns are: **-α, -ο**, e.g:

η κυρία   lady
η Κρήτη   Crete

The most common *neuter* endings are: **-ο, -ι**, e.g:

το κτίριο   building
το πορτοκάλι   orange *(fruit)*

In general, endings for plurals are as follows: masculine and feminine nouns change their endings to **-ες** (e.g. οι πατέρες, οι κυρίες) and neuter nouns change their endings to **-α** (e.g. τα κτίρια).
It must be pointed out, however, that there are many exceptions to all of the above rules.

Adjectives

Adjective endings must agree with the gender of the noun they

GRAMMAR 2

describe. You will see that in the Greek-English dictionary section of this book, all adjectives are given with their possible endings clearly marked, e.g. '**κρύος/α/ο** cold'. By far the most common adjectival endings are **-ος** for masculine, **-α** for feminine and **-ο** for neuter, e.g:

ο όμορφος άνδρας	the handsome man
η όμορφη κυρία	the beautiful lady
το όμορφο κτίριο	the beautiful building

Note that adjectives normally *precede* the verb they describe.

Verbs

The most essential Greek verbs are **είμαι** (I am, i.e. 'to be' – there is no infinitive form in Greek) and **έχω** (I have). Unlike verbs in English, Greek verbs have a different ending for each person and number.

είμαι	I am	*eeme*	έχω	I have	*ekho*
είσαι	you are	*eese*	έχεις	you have	*ekhees*
είναι	he/she/it is	*eene*	έχει	he/she/it has	*ekhee*
είμαστε	we are	*eemaste*	έχουμε	we have	*ekhoome*
είστε	you are	*eeste*	έχετε	you have	*ekhete*
είναι	they are	*eene*	έχουν	they have	*ekhoon*

NOTE: While in English it is necessary to use a personal pronoun, i.e. 'we', 'you' etc, in order to distinguish between 'we are' and 'you are' for example, in Greek this function is carried out by the different endings of the verb itself. Thus, 'I have' can be expressed in Greek as simply **έχω**, 'you are' can be expressed as simply **είσαι**, etc.

Personal pronouns

There are, however, times when the pronoun needs to be used in conjunction with the verb: if, for example, we wish to establish the sex of the person involved, i.e. 'he' or 'she', or, indeed, 'it'.

εγώ	I	*egho*
εσύ	you	*esee*
αυτός/αυτή/αυτό	he/she/it	*aftos/aftee/afto*
εμείς	we	*emees*
εσείς	you	*esees*
αυτοί/αυτές/αυτά	they (*masc./fem./neuter*)	*aftee/aftes/afta*

Thus: **αυτός έχει** = he has   **αυτή έχει** = she has, etc.

42

Streetwise

Greek has two forms of address: formal and informal. You should only use the informal σου (soo) when talking to someone you know well; the usual word for 'you' (singular or plural) is σας (sas). This is the form which normally appears in this book.

Hello/Goodbye
Γεια σας/Γεια σας
ya sas/ya sas

Good morning
Καλημέρα
kalee-mera

Good afternoon/
evening
Καλησπέρα
kalee-spera

Good night
Καληνύχτα
kalee-neekhta

How do you do?
Χαίρω πολύ
khe**ro po**lee

Pleased to meet
you
Χαίρω πολύ
khe**ro po**lee

How nice to see
you again
Χαίρομαι που σας ξαναβλέπω
***khe**ro-me poo sas ksana-**vle**po*

How are you?
Τι κάνετε;
*tee **ka**ne-te?*

Fine, thank you
Καλά, ευχαριστώ
*ka**la**, ef-kharee-**sto***

See you soon
Θα τα πούμε σύντομα
*tha ta **poo**-me **seen**-doma*

See you later
Θα σας δω αργότερα
*tha sas dho ar**gho**tera*

HAIRDRESSER'S

Streetwise

The two principal types of hairdresser's are the κουρείο (kou-**ree**o), a traditional men's barber, where you may also have a shave, and the κομμωτήριο (kommo-**tee**reeo) which is principally a women's hairdresser. Appointments are not normally necessary.

I'd like to make an appointment	**Θα ήθελα να κλείσω ραντεβού** tha **ee**thela na **klee**so ran-de**voo**
A cut and blow-dry, please	**Κούρεμα και στέγνωμα, παρακαλώ** **koo**-rema ke **stegh**-noma para-ka**lo**
A shampoo and set	**Λούσιμο και χτένισμα** **loo**-seemo ke **khte**nee-sma
Not too short	**Όχι πολύ κοντά** **o**khee po**lee** kon**da**
Not too much off the back/the fringe	**Όχι πολύ κοντά πίσω/όχι πολύ κοντή φράντζα** **o**khee po**lee** kon**da pee**so/**o**khee po**lee** kon**dee** fra**nd**-za
Take more off the top/the sides	**Κόψτε λίγο ακόμα από τα επάνω/τα πλάγια** **ko**pste **lee**gho a**ko**ma apo ta e**pa**no/ta **pla**-yee-a
My hair is permed/ My hair is tinted	**Τα μαλλιά μου έχουν περμανάντ/Τα μαλλιά μου είναι βαμμένα** ta mallee-**a** moo **ek**h-oon perma-**nand**/ta mallee-**a** moo **ee**ne va-**me**na
It's too hot	**Είναι πολύ ζεστό** **ee**-ne po**lee** zes**to**
I'd like a conditioner, please	**Θα ήθελα κοντίσιονερ, παρακαλώ** tha **ee**thela conditioner para-ka**lo**

Streetwise

When you arrive at your hotel you will be asked to fill in a registration form and your passport may be kept overnight. The cost of the room is displayed on the inside of the bedroom door. Prices quoted are normally for the room and not per person, and a service charge is normally included in the bill. Breakfast is extra. You will be expected to leave your room by noon on the day of your departure.

I have reserved a room in the name of …	Έχω κλείσει ένα δωμάτιο στο όνομα … *ekho **klee**see **e**na dhomatee-o sto **o**noma …*
I confirmed my booking by phone/ by letter	Έκανα την κράτηση από το τηλέφωνο/γραπτώς *ekana teen **kra**tee-see apo to tee**le**-fono/ghrap**tos***
What time is breakfast/dinner?	Τι ώρα είναι το πρωινό/βραδινό; *tee **o**ra **ee**-ne to pro-ee**no**/vradhee-**no**?*
Can we have breakfast in our room?	Μπορούμε να έχουμε πρωινό στο δωμάτιό μας; *bo**roo**-me na **e**khoo-me pro-ee**no** sto dho**ma**tee-**o** mas?*
Please call me at …	Παρακαλώ τηλεφωνήστε μου στις … *para-ka**lo** teele-fo**nees**te moo stees … (see **TIME**)*
Can I have my key?	Μπορώ να έχω το κλειδί μου; *bo**ro** na **e**kho to klee**dhee** moo?*
I shall be leaving tomorrow morning	Θα φύγω αύριο το πρωί *tha **fee**gho **av**ree-o to pro-**ee***

See also **ACCOMMODATION, PAYING, ROOM SERVICE**

Streetwise

Passengers may deposit luggage at left-luggage offices in major stations – look for the sign ΦΥΛΑΞΗΣ ΑΠΟΣΚΕΥΩΝ.

Where do I check in my luggage?	Πού είναι ο έλεγχος αποσκευών; *poo ee-ne o elen-khos apo-skevon?*
Where is the luggage from the London flight/train?	Πού είναι οι αποσκευές από την πτήση/το τραίνο από Λονδίνο; *poo ee-ne ee apo-skeves apo teen ptee-see/ to treno apo lon-dheeno?*
Our luggage has not arrived	Οι αποσκευές μας λείπουν *ee apo-skeves mas leepoon*
My suitcase was damaged in transit	Η βαλίτσα μου έπαθε ζημιά στη μεταφορά *ee valeet-sa moo epathe zeemee-a stee meta-fora*
Where is the left-luggage office?	Πού είναι το φύλαξης αποσκευών; *poo ee-ne to fee-laksees apo-skevon?*
Can you help me with my bags, please?	Μπορείτε να με βοηθήσετε με τις αποσκευές μου, παρακαλώ; *boree-te na me vo-eethee-se-te me tees apo-skeves moo para-kalo?*
I sent my luggage on in advance	Έχω ήδη στείλει τις αποσκευές μου *ekho eedhee steelee tees apo-skeves moo*

Streetwise

Tourist offices and some hotels will provide free maps of the town or
resort you are staying in.

Where can I buy a local map?	Από πού μπορώ να αγοράσω έναν τοπικό χάρτη; *apo poo boro na agho-raso enan topee-ko khartee?*
Have you got a town plan?	Έχετε σχέδιο της πόλης; *ekhe-te skhedhee-o tees polees?*
I want a street map of the city	Θέλω χάρτη οδών *thelo khartee odhon*
I need a road map of ...	Χρειάζομαι έναν οδικό χάρτη ... *khreee-azo-me enan odhee-ko khartee ...*
Can I get a map at the tourist office?	Μπορώ να πάρω έναν χάρτη στο τουριστικό γραφείο; *boro na paro enan khartee sto tooree-steeko ghrafee-o?*
Can you show me on the map?	Μπορείτε να μου δείξετε στο χάρτη; *boree-te na moo dheek-se-te sto khartee?*
Do you have a guide-book in English?	Έχετε οδηγό στα Αγγλικά; *ekhe-te odhee-gho sta anglee-ka?*
Do you have a guide-book to the cathedral?	Έχετε οδηγόβιβλίο για το ναό; *ekhe-te odhee-gho veevlee-o ya to na-o?*

See also **DIRECTIONS**

MEASUREMENTS

a litre of …
ένα λίτρο …
ena leetro …

a kilo of …
ένα κιλό …
ena keelo …

a pound of …
μισό κιλό …
meeso keelo …

100 grammes of …
εκατό γραμμαρία …
ekato ghramaree-a …

half a kilo of …
μισό κιλό …
meeso keelo …

a half-bottle of …
μισό μπουκάλι …
meeso bookalee …

a slice of …
μια φέτα …
mee-a feta …

a portion of …
μια μερίδα …
mee-a mereedha …

a dozen …
δώδεκα …
dhodheka …

500 drachmas worth (of …)
πεντακόσες δραχμές …
penda-ko-ses dhrakh-mes (…)

a third
ένα τρίτο
ena treeto

two thirds
δύο τρίτα
dhee-o treeta

a quarter
ένα τέταρτο
ena te-tarto

three quarters
τρία τέταρτα
tree-a te-tarta

ten per cent
δέκα στα εκατό
dheka sta ekato

more …
περισσότερο …
peree-so-tero …

less …
λιγότερο …
leegho-tero …

enough …
αρκετό …
ar-keto …

twice
δυο φορές
dhee-o fo-res

three times
τρεις φορές
trees fo-res

In most establishments you will find that the menu is in English as well as Greek.

Greeks normally eat three main meals each day:

Breakfast (**το πρόγευμα**) may be served as early as 0700. A typical breakfast will consist of toast or a roll, butter, jam and honey (particularly good) plus coffee, tea or hot chocolate. Fruit juice, eggs and cereal are optional.

Lunch (**το μεσημεριανό**) may then be eaten as late as 1300 or even 1400 since many people indulge in a midday snack of a toasted sandwich or a pastry with one of their numerous cups of Greek coffee. Lunch is usually light and will rarely consist of anything more than a dish of grilled or roast meat or fish. It is not served with cooked vegetables but with a salad which must be ordered separately. Normally, you will have a choice of **ντοματοσαλάτα** (tomato salad), **αγγουροντομάτα** (cucumber and tomato salad), or **χωριάτικη σαλάτα** (Greek salad). The latter will consist of tomato, cucumber, lettuce or white cabbage, feta cheese and olives. Salad is usually eaten with **λαδολέμονο**, a dressing of lemon and olive oil.

Dinner (**το δείπνο**) is also served relatively late, at about 1900 or 2000. If you are eating in a restaurant it would be a pity not to try a typical Greek meal. Normally this will start with **μεζέδες** (mezedes). This consists of a number of 'dips' such as **ταραμοσαλάτα** (taramosalata), **ταχίνη** (ground sesame seeds with olive oil and garlic), **χούμους** (houmous – puréed chick-pea), **τσατσίκι** (yogurt with cucumber, olive oil and mint), **καλαμάρι** (fried squid rings). (Mezedes are also often served in bars as snacks to accompany drinks.)

This is then followed by the main dish which resembles that eaten at lunchtime, i.e. meat, poultry or fish. Charcoal-grilled dishes are the best value and are normally listed under the heading **Της ώρας,** (meaning 'freshly-cooked'). Salads should be ordered separately. A third course may be served consisting of fresh fruit in season (**φρούτα**). Desserts are not normally served except as a concession to British tastes. It is however traditional to go to a patisserie (**ζαχαροπλαστείον**) for a cake after a meal.

See also **EATING OUT, ORDERING, WINES & SPIRITS**

MONEY

Streetwise

The Greek currency is the drachma. Coins of 1, 2, 5, 10, 20, 50 and 100 drachmas and notes of 100, 500, 1000 and 5000 drachmas are in circulation. There is no restriction on the amount of foreign currency or traveller's cheques which you may take into Greece but you may not take any more than 100,000 drachmas into the country or more than 20,000 drachmas out of the country.

I haven't enough money	**Δεν έχω αρκετά χρήματα** *dhen ekho ar-ke**ta khree**-mata*
Have you any change?	**Έχετε καθόλου ψιλά;** *ekhe-te katholoo psee**la**?*
Can you change a 1,000-drachma note?	**Μπορείτε να χαλάσετε ένα χιλιάρικο;** *boree-te na khala-se-te ena kheelee-areeko?*
I'd like to change these traveller's cheques	**Θα ήθελα να αλλάξω αυτά τα ταξιδιωτικά τσεκ** *tha eethela na alakso afta ta tak-seedhee-oteeka tsek*
I want to change some drachmas into pounds	**Θέλω να αλλάξω μερικές δραχμές σε λίρες** *thelo na alakso meree-kes dhrakh-mes se leeres*
What is the rate for sterling/dollars?	**Ποια είναι η ισοτιμία για τη λίρα/το δολλάριο;** *pee-a ee-ne ee eeso-teemee-a ya tee leera/to dholaree-o?*
Can I get a cash advance with my credit card?	**Μπορώ να πάρω λεφτά με την πιστωτική μου κάρτα;** *boro na paro lefta me teen peesto-teekee moo karta?*

What is there to do in the evenings?	Τι μπορούμε να κάνουμε τα βράδια; *tee boroo-me na kanoo-me ta vradhee-a?*
Where can we go to see a cabaret/go to dance?	Πού έχει καμπαρέ;/Πού χορεύουν; *poo ekhee kaba-re?/poo kho-revoon?*
Are there any good nightclubs/discos?	Υπάρχουν εδώ καλά νάιτ κλαμπ/καλές δισκοθήκες; *eepar-khoon edho kala night club/kales deeskotheekes?*
How do we get to the casino?	Πώς μπορούμε να πάμε στο καζίνο; *pos boroo-me na pa-me sto kazeeno?*
Do we need to be members?	Χρειάζεται να γίνουμε μέλη; *khree-a-ze-te na yee-noo-me melee?*
How much does it cost to get in?	Πόσο κοστίζει να μπούμε; *poso kostee-zee na boo-me?*
We'd like to reserve two seats for tonight	Θέλουμε να κλείσουμε δύο θέσεις για απόψε *theloo-me na kleesoo-me dhee-o thesees ya apop-se*
What time does the show/concert begin?	Τι ώρα αρχίζει το σόου/το κονσέρτο; *tee ora arkhee-zee to so-oo/to kon-serto?*
How long does the performance last?	Πόσο διαρκεί η παράσταση; *poso dhee-arkee ee para-stasee?*
Which film is on at the cinema?	Ποιο φιλμ έχει το σινεμά; *pee-o film ekhee to see-nema?*
Would you like to dance with me?	Θέλετε να χορέψουμε; *thelete na khorepsoome?*

See also **EATING OUT, ENTERTAINMENT**

NUMBERS

0 μηδέν mee**dhen**	11 έντεκα en-deka	30 τριάντα tree-**anda**
1 ένα ena	12 δώδεκα **dho**-dheka	40 σαράντα sa**randa**
2 δύο **dhee**-o	13 δεκατρία dheka**tree**-a	50 πενήντα pe**neenda**
3 τρία **tree**-a	14 δεκατέσσερα dheka-**te**-sera	60 εξήντα ek**seenda**
4 τέσσερα **te**-sera	15 δεκαπέντε dheka-**pen**-de	70 εβδομήντα evdho-**meenda**
5 πέντε **pen**-de	16 δεκαέξι dheka-**eksee**	80 ογδόντα ogh-**dhonda**
6 έξι **eksee**	17 δεκαεφτά dheka-e**fta**	90 ενενήντα e-ne-**neenda**
7 εφτά e**fta**	18 δεκαοχτώ dheka-okh**to**	100 εκατό e**kato**
8 οχτώ okh-**to**	19 δεκαεννέα dheka-en-**ne**-a	200 διακόσα dhee-a**kosa**
9 εννέα en-**ne**-a	20 είκοσι **ee**kosee	1000 χίλια **khee**lee-a
10 δέκα **dhe**ka	21 είκοσι ένα **ee**kosee ena	1,000,000 ένα εκατομμύριο ena ekato-**mee**ree-o

1st πρώτος **pro**tos	5th πέμπτος **pemb**-tos	9th ένατος **e**natos
2nd δεύτερος **dhef**-teros	6th έκτος **ek**tos	10th δέκατος **dhe**katos
3rd τρίτος **tree**tos	7th έβδομος **ev**-dhomos	
4th τέταρτος **te**tartos	8th όγδοος **o**gh-dho-os	

See also **MEASUREMENTS**

May we see the wine list, please?	Μπορούμε να δούμε τον κατάλογο με τα κρασιά, παρακαλώ; *boroo-me na dhoo-me ton kata-logho me ta krasee-a para-kalo?*
What do you recommend?	Τι έχετε να μας συστήσετε; *tee ekhe-te na mas seestee-se-te?*
Is there a local speciality?	Έχετε τοπική σπεσιαλιτέ; *ekhe-te topee-kee spesee-alee-te?*
How do I eat this?	Πώς το τρώω αυτό; *pos to tro-o afto?*
What is in this dish?	Τι έχει αυτό το πιάτο; *tee ekhee afto to pee-ato?*
Are the vegetables included?	Σερβίρουν και χορταρικά μαζί; *servee-roon ke khorta-reeka mazee?*
Rare/medium rare/ well done, please	Λίγο ψημένο/μέτρια ψημένο/καλοψημένο, παρακαλώ *leegho psee-meno/metree-a psee-meno/ kalopsee-meno para-kalo*
We'd like a dessert/ some coffee, please	Θα θέλαμε επιδόρπιο/καφέ, παρακαλώ *tha thela-me epee-dhorpee-o/kafe para-kalo*

PAYING

Streetwise

Credit cards are accepted in most hotels, restaurants and shops. On smaller islands they may not be accepted, however. Larger shops may also accept traveller's cheques and even foreign currency in payment, but check the exchange rate on which they base their calculations.

Can I have the bill, please?
Το λογαριασμό παρακαλώ
to logharee-asmo para-kalo

Is service/tax included?
Συμπεριλαμβάνεται και το φιλοδώρημα/ο φόρος;
seem-beree-lamva-ne-te ke to feelo-dhoreema/o foros?

How much is that?
Πόσο κάνει αυτό;
poso kanee afto?

Do I pay a deposit?
Πρέπει να δώσω προκαταβολή;
prepee na dhoso prokata-volee?

Can I pay by credit card/cheque?
Μπορώ να πληρώσω με πιστωτική κάρτα/τσεκ;
boro na plee-roso me peesto-teekee karta/tsek?

Do you accept traveller's cheques?
Δέχεστε ταξιδιωτικά τσεκ;
dhe-kheste tak-seedhee-oteeka tsek?

You've given me the wrong change
Μου έχετε δώσει λάθος ρέστα
moo ekhe-te dhosee lathos resta

I'd like a receipt/an itemized bill
Θα ήθελα απόδειξη/λεπτομερή λογαριασμό
tha eethela apo-dheeksee/lepto-meree logharee-asmo

See also **BUYING, MONEY**

My name is …

Με λένε …
*me **le**-ne …*

My date of birth is …

Έχω γεννηθεί στις …
*ekho yenee-**thee** stees …*

My address is …

Η διεύθυνσή μου είναι …
*ee dhee-**ef**-theensee moo ee-ne …*

I come from Britain/
America

Είμαι από τη Βρετανία/την Αμερική
*eeme apo tee vretanee-a/teen ameree-**kee***

I live in …

Μένω …
meno …

I work in an office/
a factory

Δουλεύω σε γραφείο/σε εργοστάσιο
*dhoo-**levo** se ghra**fee**-o/ergho-**sta**see-o*

I am a secretary/
manager

Είμαι γραμματέας/διευθυντής
*ee-me ghrama-**te**-as/dhee-ef-theen**dees***

I'm here on holiday/
business

Είμαι εδώ για διακοπές/δουλειές
*ee-me e**dho** ya dhee-ako-**pes**/dhoolee-**es***

There are four of us

Είμαστε τέσσερις
*eema-ste **te**-serees*

My daughter/My son
is six

Η κόρη μου/Ο γιος μου είναι έξι
*ee **ko**ree moo/o yos moo **ee**-ne eksee*

PETROL STATION

Streetwise

Petrol stations are to be found on all main roads. Two types of petrol are available: Regular (απλή) and Super (σούπερ). Super is more expensive but is recommended for cars. Lists of petrol stations which sell unleaded petrol are available at frontier crossings and other points of entry into Greece.

20 litres/500 drachmas (worth) of 4 star	**20 λίτρα/500 δραχμές σούπερ** *ee*ko-see **lee**tra/penda-**ko**-ses dhrakh-**mes** **soo**per
Fill it up, please	**Γεμίστε το, παρακαλώ** *ye***mee**-ste to para-ka**lo**
Check the oil/the water	**Κοιτάξτε το λάδι/νερό** kee**tak**-ste to **la**dhee/ne**ro**
Top up the windscreen washers	**Γεμίστε το νερό των καθαριστήρων** *ye***mee**-ste to ne**ro** ton katha-rees**tee**ron
Could you clean the windscreen?	**Μπορείτε να καθαρίσετε το παρμπρίζ;** bo**ree**-te na katha-**ree**se-te to par-**breez**?
A can of oil, please	**Ένα κουτί λάδι, παρακαλώ** ena koo**tee la**dhee para-ka**lo**
Where's the air line?	**Πού είναι ο αέρας;** poo **ee**-ne o a-**e**ras?
Can I have a can of petrol?	**Μπορείτε να μου δώσετε ένα μπιτόνι με βενζίνη;** bo**ree**-te na moo **dho**-se-te ena bee**to**nee me ven-**zee**nee?

See also DRIVING, PAYING

Streetwise

Films and photographic equipment are more expensive than in the UK. Photography with a hand-held camera is allowed at archaeological sites but for a tripod-mounted camera a permit is necessary. Inside museums, photography is allowed upon payment of an extra admission fee. Taking photos near military areas and airports is not permitted.

I need a colour/black and white film for this camera	Χρειάζομαι ένα έγχρωμο/ασπρόμαυρο φιλμ για αυτή τη μηχανή *khree-azo-me ena en-khromo/aspro-mavro film ya aftee tee mee-khanee*
It is for prints/slides	Είναι για φωτογραφίες/σλάιντς *ee-ne ya foto-ghrafee-es/slides*
Have you got some flash cubes for this camera?	'Εχετε φλας για αυτή τη μηχανή; *ekhe-te flas ya aftee tee mee-khanee?*
There's something wrong with my video-camera	Κάτι δεν πάει καλά με την βιντεοκάμερα *katee dhen pa-ee kala me teen veedeokamera*
The film/shutter has jammed	Το φιλμ/κουμπί έχει κολλήσει *to film/koombee ekhee kolee-see*
Can you develop this film, please?	Μπορείτε να εμφανίσετε αυτό το φιλμ, παρακαλώ; *boree-te na emfa-nee-se-te afto to film para-kalo?*
Would you take a photo of us, please?	Μας βγάζετε μία φωτογραφία, παρακαλώ; *mas vgha-ze-te mee-a foto-ghrafee-a para-kalo?*

POLICE

Streetwise

Look out for the following sign – ΑΣΤΥΝΟΜΙΑ (asteenomee-a) – 'police'. The police wear green uniforms. Tourist Police, however, wear dark grey-blue uniforms and badges (national flags) which indicate which languages they speak.

We should call the police	Πρέπει να καλέσουμε την αστυνομία **pre**pee na ka-**le**soo-me teen astee-no**mee**-a
Where is the police station?	Πού είναι το αστυνομικό τμήμα; poo **ee**-ne to astee-nomee**ko tmee**ma?
My car has been broken into	Μου διέρρηξαν το αυτοκίνητο moo dhee-**ereek**-san to afto-**kee**neeto
I've been robbed	Με λήστεψαν me **lee**step-san
How much is the fine?	Πόσο είναι το πρόστιμο; **po**so **ee**-ne to **pro**stee-mo?
Can I pay at a police station?	Μπορώ να το πληρώσω σ'ένα αστυνομικό τμήμα; bo**ro** na to plee-**ro**so **se**na astee-nomee**ko tmee**ma?
I don't have my driving licence on me	Δεν έχω μαζί μου την άδεια οδήγησης dhen **ekho** ma**zee** moo teen **adhee**-a o**dhee**-yeesees
I didn't know the regulations	Δεν ήξερα τους κανονισμούς dhen **eek**-sera toos kano-nees**moos**

Streetwise

Stamps can also be bought at kiosks and shops which sell postcards, although they may be more expensive in these places. Post boxes are yellow. Most post offices are open 0800-1430/1500.

How much is a letter to England/ America?	**Πόσο κάνει ένα γράμμα για την Αγγλία/Αμερική;** *po*so *ka*nee *e*na **ghra**ma ya teen anglee-a/ ame-reekee?*
I'd like six stamps for postcards to Great Britain, please	**Θα ήθελα έξι γραμματόσημα για κάρτες στην Αγγλία παρακαλώ** *tha ee-thela eksee ghrama-toseema ya kar-tes steen anglee-a para-kalo*
Twelve 35-drachma stamps, please	**Δώδεκα γραμματόσημα των τριάντα πέντε, παρακαλώ** **dho**-deka ghrama-**to**seema ton tree-**a**nda **pen**-de para-ka**lo**
I want to send a telegram to …	**Θέλω να στείλω ένα τηλεγράφημα …** *the*lo na *stee*lo *e*na teele-**ghra**feema …*
How much will it cost?	**Πόσο θα κοστίσει;** *po*so tha kos**tee**-see?*
I want to send this parcel	**Θέλω να στείλω αυτό το δέμα** *the*lo na *stee*lo afto to **dhe**ma*
I'd like to make a telephone call	**Θέλω να κάνω ένα τηλεφώνημα** *the*lo na *ka*no *e*na tee-lefo-neema*

PROBLEMS

Can you help me, please?	Μπορείτε να με βοηθήσετε σας παρακαλώ; *boree-te na me vo-eethee-se-te sas para-kalo?*
What is the matter?	Τι συμβαίνει; *tee seem-venee?*
I am in trouble	Έχω πρόβλημα *ekho prov-leema*
I don't understand	Δεν καταλαβαίνω *dhen kata-laveno*
Do you speak English?	Μιλάτε Αγγλικά; *meela-te anglee-ka?*
Please repeat that	Επαναλαμβάνετε παρακαλώ; *epana-lam-va-ne-te para-kalo?*
I have run out of money	Δεν έχω άλλα λεφτά *dhen ekho ala lefta*
I have lost my way	Έχω χαθεί *ekho kha-thee*
I have forgotten my passport	Ξέχασα το διαβατήριό μου *kse-khasa to dhee-avateeree-o moo*
Please give me my passport back	Το διαβατήριό μου παρακαλώ *to dhee-avateeree-o moo para-kalo*
Where is the British Consulate?	Πού είναι το Βρετανικό Προξενείο; *poo ee-ne to vreta-neeko prok-senee-o?*
Leave me alone	Αφήστε με ήσυχο *afeeste me eeseekho*

See also **ACCIDENTS, COMPLAINTS, EMERGENCIES, POLICE**

PRONUNCIATION 1

In the pronunciation system used in this book, Greek sounds are represented by spellings of the nearest possible sounds in English. Hence, when you read out the pronunciation – the phrase in *italics* after the Greek phrase or word – sound the letters as if you were reading an English word. The syllable to be stressed is shown in **heavy italics**. The following notes should help you:

	REMARKS	EXAMPLE	PRONOUNCED
gh	like a rough g	γάλα	***gh**ala*
dh	like *th* in *this*	δάκτυλος	***dha**k-teelos*
th	like *th* in *thin*	θέατρο	***the**-atro*
ks	like *x* in *fox*	ξένος	***ks**enos*
r	slightly trilled *r*	ρόδα	*rodha*
kh	like *ch* in *loch*	χάνω	***kh**ano*
	or like a rough *h*	χέρι	***kh**eree*
ps	like *ps* in *lapse*	ψάρι	***ps**aree*

Greek spelling is very regular and if you can master the alphabet you may find yourself reading straight from the translations. The alphabet is as follows:

GREEK LETTER	CLOSEST ENGLISH SOUND	SHOWN BY	EXAMPLE	
Α, α	*hand*	a	άνθρωπος	*an-thropos*
Β, β	*vine*	v	βούτυρο	*voo-teero*
Γ, γ	*see above*	gh	γάλα	*ghala*
	or yes	y	για	*ya*
Δ, δ	*this*	dh	δάκτυλος	*dhak-teelos*
Ε, ε	*met*	e	έτοιμος	*e-teemos*
Ζ, ζ	*zone*	z	ζώνη	*zonee*
Η, η	*meet*	ee	ήλιος	*ee-leeos*
Θ, θ	*thin*	th	θέατρο	*the-atro*
Ι, ι	*meet*	ee	ίππος	*eepos*
Κ, κ	*key*	k	και	*ke*

PRONUNCIATION 2

GREEK LETTER	CLOSEST ENGLISH SOUND	SHOWN BY	EXAMPLE	
Λ, λ	log	l	λάδι	*ladhee*
Μ, μ	mat	m	μάτι	*matee*
Ν, ν	not	n	νύχτα	*neekh-ta*
Ξ, ξ	rocks	ks	ξένος	*ksenos*
Ο, ο	cot	o	όχι	*okhee*
Π, π	pat	p	πόλη	*polee*
Ρ, ρ	carrot	r	ρόδα	*rodha*
Σ, σ (, ς)	sat	s	σήμα	*seema*
Τ, τ	top	t	τράπεζα	*tra-peza*
Υ, υ	meet	ee	ύπνος	*eepnos*
Φ, φ	fat	f	φούστα	*foosta*
Χ, χ	see above	kh	χάνω	*khano*
		kh	χέρι	*kheree*
Ψ, ψ	lapse	ps	ψάρι	*psaree*
Ω, ω	cot	o	ώρα	*ora*

There are a few combinations of letters which you might find tricky:

αι	met	e	γυναίκα	*ghee-neka*
αυ	café	af	αυτό	*afto*
	or have	av	αύριο	*av-reeo*
γγ	angle	ng	Αγγλία	*anglee-a*
γκ	get	g	γκάζι	*gazee*
μπ	bag	b	μπλούζα	*blooza*
οι	meet	ee	πλοίο	*plee-o*
ου	moon	oo	ούζο	*oozo*

You will notice from the phrases that a Greek question mark is the same as an English semi-colon.

Streetwise

Note that Good Friday, Easter Monday and the first Monday in Lent depend on the date of Easter in the Greek Orthodox calendar; this only occasionally coincides with Easter at home. You may also come across local holidays and festivals.

St Basil's Day	January 1st
Epiphany	January 6th
Lent Holiday	first Monday in Lent
Good Friday	
Easter Monday	
Independence Day	March 25th
May Day	May 1st
Assumption Day	August 15th
Ochi Day	October 28th
Christmas Day	December 25th
Gathering of the Virgin Mary	December 26th

Streetwise

Children under 4 travel free; children between 4 and 12 pay half fare. Booking your seat in advance is recommended.

What time are the trains to …?	Τι ώρα φεύγουν τα τραίνα για …; *tee ora fev-ghoon ta trena ya …?*
When is the next train to …?	Πότε είναι το επόμενο τραίνο για …; *po-te ee-ne to epo-meno treno ya …?*
What time does it get there?	Τι ώρα φτάνει εκεί; *tee ora ftanee ekee?*
Do I have to change?	Πρέπει να αλλάξω; *prepee na alakso?*
A return to …, first class	Με επιστροφή για …, πρώτη θέση *me epee-strofee ya …, protee thesee*
A single to …, second class	Απλή διαδρομή για …, δεύτερη θέση *aplee dhee-adhromee ya …, dhef-teree thesee*
I want to reserve a seat in a non-smoking compartment	Θέλω να κλείσω θέση σε βαγόνι μη καπνιζόντων *thelo na kleeso thesee se vaghonee mee kapnee-zondon*
I want to reserve a couchette/sleeper	Θέλω να κλείσω κουκέτα/βαγκόν-λι *thelo na kleeso koo-keta/vagon-lee*

See also **LUGGAGE, TRAIN TRAVEL**

I have broken a glass/the window	Έσπασα ένα ποτήρι/το παράθυρο *espasa ena potee-ree/to para-theero*
There is a hole in my shoe/these trousers	Υπάρχει μία τρύπα στο παπούτσι μου/σ'αυτό το παντελόνι *eepar-khee mee-a treepa sto pa-pootsee moo/ safto to pan-de-lonee*
This is broken/torn	Έχει σπάσει/σχιστεί *ekhee spasee/skheestee*
Can you repair this?	Μπορείτε να το διορθώσετε αυτό; *boree-te na to dhee-ortho-se-te afto?*
Can you do it quickly?	Μπορείτε να το ετοιμάσετε γρήγορα; *boree-te na to eteema-se-te ghree-ghora?*
When can you get it done by?	Πότε μπορείτε να το έχετε έτοιμο; *po-te boree-te na to ekhe-te etee-mo?*
I need some adhesive tape/a safety pin?	Θέλω λίγο σελλοτέιπ/μία παραμάνα *thelo leegho selote-eep/mee-a para-mana*
This handle has come off	Έχει βγει το χερούλι *ekhee vyee to kheroo-lee*

See also **ACCIDENTS, BREAKDOWNS, EMERGENCIES**

ROAD CONDITIONS

Streetwise

On certain sections of motorway you may find that you have to pay a toll. These charges are normally fairly low, however.

Is there a route that avoids the traffic?
Υπάρχει παράκαμψη για την κίνηση;
eepar-khee parakamp-see ya teen keenee-see?

Is the traffic heavy on the motorway?
Έχει κίνηση ο αυτοκινητόδρομος;
ekhee keenee-see o afto-keeneeto-dhromos?

What is causing this hold-up?
Τι προκαλεί τη συμφόρηση;
tee pro-kalee tee seem-foreesee?

When will the road be clear?
Πότε θα ανοίξει ο δρόμος;
po-te tha aneek-see o dhromos?

Is there a detour?
Υπάρχει παράκαμψη;
eepar-khee parakamp-see?

Is the road to ... snowed up?
Έχει χιόνια στο δρόμο για ...;
ekhee khee-onee-a sto dhromo ya ...?

Do I need chains?
Χρειάζομαι αλυσίδες;
khree-azo-me alee-seedhes?

See also DRIVING, WEATHER

Come in!	**Περάστε** *pe**ras**-te*
We'd like breakfast/ a bottle of wine in our room	**Θα θέλαμε πρωινό/ένα μπουκάλι κρασί** **στο δωμάτιό μας** *tha **the**la-me pro-ee**no**/ena boo-**ka**lee kra**see** sto* *dho**ma**tee-**o** mas*
Put it on my bill	**Βάλτε το στο λογαριασμό μου** ***val**-te to sto logharee-as**mo** moo*
I'd like an outside line, please	**Συνδέστε με με εξωτερική γραμμή** **παρακαλώ** *seen-**dhes**-te me me ekso-teree**kee** ghra**mee*** *para-ka**lo***
I have locked myself out of my room	**Κλειδώθηκα έξω** *klee**dho**-thee-ka **e**kso*
Where is the socket for my electric razor?	**Πού είναι η πρίζα για την ξυριστική** **μου μηχανή;** *poo **ee**-ne ee **pree**za ya teen kseeree-stee**kee*** *moo mee-kha**nee**?*
What's the voltage?	**Πόσα βολτ είναι το ρεύμα;** ***po**sa volt **ee**-ne to **rev**ma?*
May I have an extra blanket/pillow?	**Μπορώ να έχω μία ακόμα κουβέρτα/ένα** **ακόμα μαξιλάρι;** *bo**ro** na **e**kho **mee**-a a**ko**ma koo-**ver**ta/ena* *a**ko**ma maksee-**la**ree?*
Please send someone to collect my luggage	**Παρακαλώ στείλτε κάποιον να** **παραλάβει τις αποσκευές μου** *para-ka**lo**, **steel**-te **ka**pee-on na para-**la**vee tees* *apo-ske**ves** moo*

See also **CLEANING, COMPLAINTS, HOTEL DESK, TELEPHONE**

SELF-CATERING

We've booked an apartment in the name of ...

'Εχουμε κλείσει ένα διαμέρισμα στο όνομα ...
*ekhoo-me **klee**see **e**na dhee-a-**me**rees-ma sto **o**noma ...*

Which is the key for the front door?

Ποιο είναι το κλειδί της μπροστινής πόρτας;
*pee-o **ee**-ne to klee**dhee** tees brostee-**nees portas**?*

Where is the electricity meter/the water heater?

Πού είναι ο μετρητής του ηλεκτρικού/ο θερμοσίφωνας;
*poo **ee**-ne o metree-**tees** too eelek-tree**koo**/o thermo-**see**fonas?*

How does the heating/the shower work?

Πώς λειτουργεί το καλοριφέρ/το ντους;
*pos leetoor-**yee** to kalo-ree**fer**/to doos?*

Which day does the cleaner come?

Ποια μέρα έρχεται η καθαρίστρια;
*pee-a **me**ra er-khe-te ee katha-**rees**tree-a?*

A fuse has blown

Κάηκε κάποια ασφάλεια
*ka-ee-ke **ka**pee-a as**fa**lee-a*

Where can I contact you?

Πού μπορώ να σας βρω;
*poo bo**ro** na sas vro?*

Streetwise

Shops are normally open 0930-1730, Mon.-Sat. In popular tourist areas shops may remain open till late in the evening. You can haggle over prices in most smaller shops but not in department stores.

Where is the main shopping area?	Πού είναι η αγορά; *poo **ee**-ne ee agho-**ra**?*
Where are the big stores?	Πού είναι τα πολυκαταστήματα; *poo **ee**-ne ta polee-kata-**stee**mata?*
What time do the shops close?	Τι ώρα κλείνουν τα μαγαζιά; *tee ora **klee**noon ta maghazee-**a**?*
How much does that cost?	Πόσο κοστίζει εκείνο εκεί; *po so kos**tee**-zee e**kee**-no e**kee**?*
How much is it per kilo/per metre?	Πόσο κάνει το κιλό/το μέτρο; *po so **ka**nee to **kee**lo/to **me**tro?*
Can I try it on?	Μπορώ να το προβάρω; *bo**ro** na to pro**va**ro?*
Where is the shoe/food department?	Πού είναι το τμήμα παπουτσιών/τροφών; *poo **ee**-ne to tmeema pa-pootsee-**on**/trofon?*
I'm looking for a gift for my wife	Γυρεύω ένα δώρο για τη γυναίκα μου *yee-**revo** ena **dho**ro ya tee yee-**ne**ka moo*
I'm just looking	Απλώς βλέπω *ap**los** vlepo*

See also **BUYING, PAYING**

SIGHTSEEING

Streetwise

The opening hours of archaeological sites and museums are subject to alteration at short notice. As a rule, however, museums and sites remain closed on Tuesdays, except for the National Archaeological Museum in Athens which closes on Monday. All close on public holidays. Reductions for students are available on the production of an identity card and there are also reductions for children.

What is there to see here?	Τι μπορούμε να δούμε εδώ; *tee boroo-me na dhoo-me edho?*
Where is the museum/the main square?	Πού είναι το μουσείο/η κεντρική πλατεία; *poo ee-ne to moosee-o/ee kendree-kee platee-a?*
What time does the guided tour begin?	Τι ώρα αρχίζει η ξενάγηση; *tee ora arkhee-zee ee ksena-yeesee?*
What time does the museum open?	Τι ώρα ανοίγει το μουσείο; *tee ora anee-yee to moosee-o?*
Is the castle open to the public?	Είναι το κάστρο ανοιχτό στο κοινό; *ee-ne to kastro aneekh-to sto keeno?*
How much does it cost to get in?	Πόσο κάνει η είσοδος; *poso kanee ee eeso-dhos?*
Is there a reduction for children/senior citizens?	Έχει έκπτωση για παιδιά/ συνταξιούχους; *ekhee ek-ptosee ya pedhee-a/ seen-daksee-ookhoos?*
Where can I buy a film?	Πού μπορώ να αγοράσω ένα φιλμ; *poo boro na agho-raso ena film?*

See also **MAPS & GUIDES, TRIPS & EXCURSIONS**

Streetwise

You can buy cigarettes from roadside kiosks, which also sell newspapers and stamps. The 'no smoking' sign is ΑΠΑΓΟΡΕΥΕΤΑΙ ΤΟ ΚΑΠΝΙΣΜΑ.

Do you mind if I smoke?	**Σας πειράζει να καπνίσω;** *sas pee-razee na kap-neeso?*
May I have an ashtray?	**Μπορώ να έχω ένα τασάκι;** *boro na ekho ena ta-sakee?*
Is this a no-smoking area/compartment?	**Είναι αυτός ο χώρος/αυτό το διαμέρισμα για μη καπνίζοντες;** *ee-ne aftos o khoros/afto to dhe-a-mereesma ya mee kapnee-zon-des?*
A packet of ..., please	**Ένα πακέτο ..., παρακαλώ** *ena paketo ..., para-kalo*
Have you any American/English brands?	**Έχετε αμερικάνικα/αγγλικά τσιγάρα;** *ekhe-te ameree-kaneeka/anglee-ka tsee-ghara?*
I'd like some pipe tobacco	**Θα ήθελα καπνό** *tha eethela kapno*
Have you a gas refill for my lighter?	**Έχετε αέριο για τον αναπτήρα μου;** *ekhe-te a-eree-o ya ton anap-teera moo?*
Have you got a light ?	**Μήπως έχετε φωτιά;** *meepos ekhe-te fotee-a?*

SPORTS

| Which sports activities are available here? | Τι σπορ έχει εδώ; |
| | *tee spor ekhee edho?* |

Is it possible to go
fishing/riding?

Μπορούμε να πάμε για ψάρεμα/για
ιππασία;
boroo-me na pa-me ya psa-rema/ya eepasee-a?

Where can we play
tennis/golf?

Πού μπορούμε να παίξουμε τένις/γκολφ;
poo booroo-me na peksoo-me tennis/golf?

Are there any
interesting walks
nearby?

Υπάρχει καλό μέρος για περίπατο εδώ
κοντά;
*eepar-khee kalo meros ya peree-pato edho
konda?*

Can we rent the
equipment?

Μπορούμε να νοικιάσουμε τον
εξοπλισμό;
boroo-me na neekee-asoo-me ton eksopleesmo?

Do we need to be
members?

Πρέπει να είμαστε μέλη;
prepee na eema-ste melee?

Can we take
lessons?

Μπορούμε να πάρουμε μαθήματα;
boroo-me na paroo-me mathee-mata?

See also **BEACH, ENTERTAINMENT, WATERSPORTS, WINTER SPORTS**

Streetwise

In most towns you will find taxis in the main square. Taxis in Athens are yellow and labelled 'TAXI' or 'ΤΑΞΙ'. Try and get an idea of how much the journey should cost beforehand.

Can you order me a taxi?	Μπορείτε να μου φωνάξετε ένα ταξί; *bo***ree**-te na moo fo**nak**-se-te **e**na tak**see**?
To the main station/airport, please	Στο σταθμό/αεροδρόμιο, παρακαλώ *sto stath-**mo**/aero-**dhro**mee-o para-ka**lo***
Take me to this address	Σ' αυτή τη διεύθυνση *saf**tee** tee dhee-**ef**-theensee*
Is it far?	Είναι μακριά; ***ee**-ne makree-**a**?*
How much will it cost?	Πόσο θα κοστίσει; *po***so** tha kos**tee**-see?
Can you wait here for a few minutes?	Μπορείτε να περιμένετε εδώ για λίγα λεπτά; *bo***ree**-te na peree-**me**-ne-te e**dho** ya **lee**gha lep**ta**?
Turn left/right here	Στρίψτε αριστερά/δεξιά εδώ *streep*-ste aree-ste**ra**/dhek**see**-**a** e**dho***
Please stop here/at the corner	Σταματήστε εδώ/στη γωνία σας παρακαλώ *stama-**tee**-ste e**dho**/stee gho**nee**-a sas para-ka**lo***
How much is it?	Πόσο κάνει; *po***so ka**nee?
Keep the change	Κρατήστε τα ρέστα *kra**tee**-ste ta **re**sta*

Streetwise

The Greek telephone and telegraph services are the responsibility of the OTE (Οργανισμός Τηλεπικοινωνιών Ελλάδος) which is separate from the Post Office. You will find their offices in all towns and villages. At these offices you can use a booth to make your call and then pay afterwards at the counter. Be prepared to queue, especially from 2100 onwards when cheap rates operate. Local calls and long-distance calls can also be made from hotels and from phone booths (περίπτερα *pereeptera*) in restaurants, hotels and post offices. The dialling code for the UK is 0044.

I want to make a phone call	Θέλω να τηλεφωνήσω *thelo na tee-lefo-neeso*
Can I have a line?	Μου δίνετε γραμμή; *moo dhee-ne-te ghramee?*
I would like …	Θα ήθελα το … *tha eethela to … (see NUMBERS)*
I want to reverse the charges	Θέλω να κάνω κλήση πληρωτέα από τον παραλήπτη *thelo na kano kleesee pleerotea apo ton paraleeptee*
Have you got change for the phone?	Έχετε ψιλά για το τηλέφωνο; *ekhe-te pseela ya to teele-fono?*
What coins do I need?	Τι κέρματα χρειάζομαι; *tee kermata khree-azo-me?*
How much is it to phone Britain/the USA?	Πόσο κάνει ένα τηλεφώνημα στην Βρετανία/στις Ηνωμένες Πολιτείες; *poso kanee ena tee-lefo-neema stee vretanee-a/ stees eeno-me-nes poleetee-es?*

I can't get through

Δεν μπορώ να πιάσω γραμμή
dhen boro na pee-aso ghramee

The line's engaged

Ο αριθμός μιλάει
o areethmos meela-ee

Hello, this is …

Εμπρός … εδώ
embros, … edho

Can I speak to …?

Μπορώ να μιλήσω στον …;
boro na mee-leeso ston …?

I've been cut off

Μας κόψανε
mas kopsa-ne

It's a bad line

Δεν ακούω καθαρά
dhen akoo-o katha-ra

YOU MAY HEAR:

Περιμένετε
peree-me-ne-te

Hold the line

Λυπάμαι, μιλάει
leepa-me, meela-ee

I'm sorry, it's engaged

Παρακαλώ προσπαθείστε πάλι αργότερα
para-kalo prospa-thee-ste palee argho-tera

Please try again later

Ποιος είναι στο τηλέφωνο;
pee-os ee-ne sto tee-lefono?

Who's calling?

Συγνώμη, λάθος αριθμός
seegh-nomee, lathos areethmos

Sorry, wrong number

What's the time?	Τι ώρα είναι; *tee ora eene?*
It's ...	Είναι ... *eene ...*

8.00	οχτώ η ώρα *okh-to ee ora*
8.05	οχτώ και πέντε *okh-to ke pen-de*
8.10	οχτώ και δέκα *okh-to ke dheka*
8.15	οχτώ και τέταρτο *okh-to ke te-tarto*
8.20	οχτώ και είκοσι *okh-to ke ee-kosee*
8.25	οχτώ και είκοσι πέντε *okh-to ke ee-kosee pen-de*
8.30	οχτώμιση *okh-tomeesee*
8.35	εννέα παρά είκοσι πέντε *e-ne-a para ee-kosee pen-de*
8.40	εννέα παρά είκοσι *e-ne-a para ee-kosee*
8.45	εννέα παρά τέταρτο *e-ne-a para te-tarto*
8.50	εννέα παρά δέκα *e-ne-a para dheka*
8.55	εννέα παρά πέντε *e-ne-a para pen-de*
12.00	δώδεκα η ώρα *dho-dheka ee ora*

When?	Τι ώρα; *tee ora?*
What time do you open?	Τι ώρα ανοίγετε; *tee ora anee-ye-te?*
How long will it take to get there?	Πόσην ώρα για να φτάσουμε εκεί; *poseen ora ya na ftasoo-me ekee?*
We can be there in half an hour	Μπορούμε να είμαστε εκεί σε μισή ώρα *boroo-me na eemas-te ekee se meesee ora*
We arrived early/late	Φτάσαμε νωρίς/αργά *ftasa-me norees/argha*
Two hours ago	Πριν δύο ώρες *preen dhee-o o-res*
Before ... o'clock	Πριν τις ... *preen tees ... (see TIME)*
At about half past three	Κατά τις τρεισήμιση *kata tees trees-eemeesee*
In the morning/In the afternoon	Το πρωί/Το απόγευμα *to pro-ee/to apo-yevma*
The table is booked for ... this evening	Το τραπέζι είναι κλεισμένο για ... το βράδυ *to tra-pezee ee-ne klees-meno ya ... (see TIME)* *to vradhee*

TIPPING

Streetwise

Tipping is normally on a small scale in Greece. The maximum is 10% for waiters in large restaurants, and perhaps between 100 and 200 drachmas in smaller establishments. In bars it is quite acceptable to leave just a few coins. You should also tip cinema and theatre usherettes, guides and parking attendants. A suggested figure is 100 drachmas. There is already a flat fee included in taxi fares so generally there is no need to tip taxi drivers.

Sorry, I don't have any change	**Συγνώμη, δεν έχω ψιλά** *seegh-**no**mee, dhen **e**kho psee**la***
Could you give me change of ...?	**Μπορείτε να μου χαλάσετε ...;** *bo**ree**-te na moo kha**la**-se-te ...?*
Is it usual to tip ...?	**Συνηθίζεται να δίνει κανείς φιλοδώρημα ...;** *seenee-**thee**-ze-te na **dhee**nee ka**nees** feelo-**dho**reema ...?*
How much should I tip?	**Πόσο πρέπει να δώσω για φιλοδώρημα;** *po*so *pre*pee na *dho*so ya feelo-**dho**reema?*
Is the tip included?	**Συμπεριλαμβάνεται και το φιλοδώρημα;** *seem-bereelam-**va**-ne-te ke to feelo-**dho**reema?*
Keep the change	**Κρατήστε τα ρέστα** *kra**tee**-ste ta **re**sta*
Make it ... drachmas	**Κρατήστε ... δραχμές** *kra**tee**ste ... (see **NUMBERS**) dhrakh**mes***

See also **EATING OUT, TAXIS**

Streetwise

Public toilets are few and far between in towns but it's customary to use the toilets in hotels, restaurants and cafés. It is wise to carry tissues or toilet paper with you.

Where is the Gents'/ the Ladies'?	Πού είναι των ανδρών/γυναικών; *poo **ee**-ne ton andh**ron**/yee-ne**kon**?*
Do you have to pay?	Πρέπει να πληρώσω; ***pre**pee na plee-**ro**so?*
This toilet does not flush	Δεν τρέχει το καζανάκι *dhen **tre**khee to kaza-**na**kee*
There is no toilet paper/soap	Δεν έχει χαρτί/σαπούνι *dhen **e**khee khar**tee**/sa**poo**-nee*
Is there a toilet for the disabled?	Υπάρχει τουαλέτα για ανάπηρους; *ee**par**-khee too-a-**le**ta ya a**na**-peeroos?*
Are there facilities for mothers with babies?	Υπάρχουν ευκολίες για μητέρες με μωρά; *eepar-**khoon** ef-ko**lee**-es ya mee-**te**-res me mo**ra**?*
The towels have run out	Τέλειωσαν οι πετσέτες ***te**lee-osan ee pe**tse**-tes*

TRAIN TRAVEL

Is this the train for ...?

Είναι αυτό το τραίνο για ...;
ee-ne afto to treno ya ...?

Is this seat free?

Είναι ελεύθερη αυτή η θέση;
ee-ne elef-theree aftee ee thesee?

I have a seat reservation

Έχω κλείσει θέση
ekho kleesee thesee

Can you help me put my suitcase in the luggage rack?

Μπορείτε να με βοηθήσετε να βάλω τη βαλίτσα μου επάνω;
boree-te na me vo-eethee-se-te na valo tee valeet-sa moo epano?

May I open the window?

Μπορώ να ανοίξω το παράθυρο;
boro na aneek-so to para-theero?

What time do we get to ...?

Τι ώρα φτάνουμε ...;
tee ora ftanoo-me ...?

Is there a restaurant car?

Υπάρχει εστιατόριο;
eepar-khee estee-atoree-o?

This is a no-smoking compartment

Εδώ είναι το μη καπνιζόντων
edho ee-ne to mee kapnee-zondon

Tell me when we get to ...

Πέστε μου όταν φτάσουμε ...
pes-te moo otan ftasoo-me ...

See also **LUGGAGE, RAILWAY STATION**

What's the best way to get to …?
Ποιος είναι ο καλύτερος τρόπος για να πάω …;
*pee-os **ee**-ne o ka**lee**-teros **tro**pos ya na **pa**-o …?*

How much is it to fly to …?
Πόσο κάνει το αεροπορικό εισιτήριο για …;
*po*so **ka**nee to aero-poree**ko** eesee-**tee**ree-o ya …?*

Are there any special cheap fares?
Έχετε φτηνά εισιτήρια;
*ekhe-te **fteena** eesee-**tee**ree-a?*

What time is the train/flight?
Τι ώρα είναι το τραίνο/η πτήση;
*tee ora **ee**-ne to **tre**no/ee **ptee**-see?*

Can I change my booking?
Μπορώ να αλλάξω το εισιτήριό μου;
*boro na a**lakso** to eesee-**tee**ree-o moo?*

Can you book me on the London flight?
Μπορείτε να μου κρατήσετε θέση για την πτήση στο Λονδίνο;
*boree-te na moo kra**tee**-se-te **the**see ya teen **ptee**see sto lon-**dhee**no?*

Can I get back to Manchester tonight?
Μπορώ να επιστρέψω στο Μάντσεστερ απόψε;
*boro na epee-**strepso** sto Manchester a**pop**-se?*

Two second-class returns to …
Δύο με επιστροφή, δεύτερη θέση για …
dhee-o me epee-stro**fee**, **dhef**-teree **the**see ya …*

Can you book me into a hotel?
Μπορείτε να μου κλείσετε ξενοδοχείο;
*boree-te na moo **klee**-se-te kseno-dho**khee**-o?*

Do you do bookings for shows/concerts?
Κλείνετε θέσεις για σόου/συναυλίες;
*klee-ne-te **the**sees ya **so**-oo/seenav**lee**-es?*

TRIPS & EXCURSIONS

Are there any
sightseeing tours?

Υπάρχουν περιοδείες στα αξιοθέατα;
*eepar-khoon peree-o**dhee**-es sta aksee-o**the**-ata?*

How long does the
tour take?

Πόσην ώρα κρατάει η περιοδεία;
***po**seen **o**ra kra**ta**-ee ee peree-o**dhee**-a?*

Are there any guided
tours of the temple?

Υπάρχουν ξεναγήσεις του ναού;
*eepar-khoon ksena-**yee**sees too na-**oo**?*

Is there a reduction
for a group?

Κάνετε έκπτωση σε ομάδες;
ka-ne-te **e**k-ptosee se o**ma**dhes?

Is there a reduction
for senior citizens/
children?

Κάνετε έκπτωση σε συνταξιούχους/
παιδιά;
ka-ne-te **e**k-ptosee se seen-daksee-**oo**khoos/
pedhee-**a**?

Where do we stop
for lunch?

Πού σταματάμε για μεσημεριανό;
*poo stama-**ta**-me ya mesee-meree-a**no**?*

Please stop the bus,
my child is feeling
sick

Παρακαλώ σταματήστε το λεωφορείο, το
παιδί μου θέλει εμετό
*para-ka**lo** stama-**tee**-ste to leo-fo**ree**-o, to pe**dhee**
moo **the**lee eme**to**

See also **SIGHTSEEING**

Is it possible to go water-skiing/ windsurfing?

Μπορώ να πάω για σκι/γουίντ-σερφ;

boro na pa-o ya ski/windsurf?

Can we rent a motorboat?

Μπορούμε να νοικιάσουμε μία βάρκα με μηχανή;

boroo-me na neekee-asoo-me mee-a varka me mee-khanee?

Can one swim in the river?

Μπορεί κανείς να κολυμπήσει στο ποτάμι;

boree kanees na koleem-beesee sto pota-mee?

Can we fish here?

Μπορούμε να ψαρέψουμε εδώ;

boroo-me na psarep-soo-me edho?

Is there a paddling pool for the children?

Υπάρχει λιμνούλα για τα παιδιά;

eepar-khee leem-noola ya ta pedhee-a?

Do you give lessons?

Παραδίδετε μαθήματα;

paradhee-dhe-te mathee-mata?

Where is the municipal swimming pool?

Πού είναι η δημοτική πισίνα;

poo ee-ne ee dheemoteekee peeseena?

Is it an outdoor pool?

Είναι ανοιχτή;

ee-ne aneekh-tee?

See also **BEACH**

Streetwise

A north wind, 'the Meltemi', blows throughout the Aegean from July to September. Be prepared for long delays as ferries take shelter.

It's a lovely day	Είναι υπέροχη μέρα *ee-ne ee-perokhee mera*
What dreadful weather!	Τι απαίσιος καιρός! *tee a-pesee-os keros!*
It is raining/It is snowing	Βρέχει/Χιονίζει *vrekhee/khee-oneezee*
It's windy/sunny/foggy	Έχει αέρα/ήλιο/ομίχλη *ekhee a-era/eelee-o/omeekh-lee*
There's a nice breeze blowing	Έχει ένα ευχάριστο αεράκι *ekhee ena ef-kharee-sto a-erakee*
Will it be cold tonight?	Θα κάνει κρύο απόψε; *tha kanee kree-o apop-se?*
Is it going to rain/to snow?	Θα βρέξει;/Θα χιονίσει; *tha vreksee?/tha khee-oneesee?*
Will there be a frost?	Θα κάνει παγωνιά; *tha kanee paghonee-a?*
Will there be a thunderstorm?	Θα έχει καταιγίδα; *tha ekhee ka-te-yeedha?*
Is it going to be fine?	Θα κάνει καλό καιρό; *tha kanee kalo kero?*

In Greece and Cyprus wine is drunk with meals but is not as popular as in other European countries. There is a wide variety of wines to suit all tastes and although, quality-wise, few are outstanding, most are very reasonable. Furthermore, prices are generally low so it won't cost a fortune to sample a number of different wines.

Many of the local wines tend to be on the sweet side and be warned that when a wine is described as **γλυκύ**, i.e. sweet, it may well be very sweet. So, if you don't like sweet wine, make sure you ask the waiter for **ξηρό κρασί** (*kseero krasee* – dry wine).

You may find the following terms helpful:

κρασί	wine	*krasee*
άσπρο	white	*aspro*
ερυθρό	red	*ereethro*
ροζέ	rosé	*roze*
γλυκύ	sweet	*ghleekee*
ξηρό	dry	*kseero*
αφρώδες	sparkling	*aphrodhes*

Thus,	άσπρο γλυκύ	sweet white wine	*aspro ghleekee*
	ξηρό ερυθρό	dry red wine	*kseero ereethro*

Ρετσίνα – *retseena* – which has come to be known as the 'national' wine of Greece – is a resinated, white, dry wine of which there are a number of brands, and which is well worth trying.
Many of the islands produce their own local wines and asking the waiter for a recommendation, specifying the type of wine you prefer, is not a bad idea.

Most well-known brands of spirits are available in Greece. The best-known Greek spirit is of course *ouzo*, a strong aniseed-flavoured drink which is normally mixed with water and ice. Greek brandy, *metaxa*, is sweeter and harsher than the French equivalent and is graded from one to seven stars according to the quality.

WINES & SPIRITS 2

We'd like an aperitif

Θα θέλαμε απεριτίφ
*tha **the**la-me aperee-**teef***

May I have the wine list, please?

Μπορώ να έχω τον κατάλογο με τα κρασιά, παρακαλώ;
*bo**ro** na **e**kho ton ka**ta**-logho me ta krasee-**a** para-ka**lo**?*

Can you recommend a good red/white/ rosé wine?

Έχετε να μας συστήσετε ένα καλό κόκκινο/άσπρο/ροζέ κρασί;
*ekhe-te na mas see**stee**-se-te **e**na ka**lo** ko**kee**-no/ aspro/ro-**ze** kra**see**?*

A jug of retsina

Μία κανάτα ρετσίνα
***mee**-a ka**na**ta ret-**see**na*

A half-bottle of ...

Μικρό μπουκάλι ...
*mee**kro** boo-ka**lee** ...*

This wine is not chilled

Αυτό το κρασί δεν είναι κρύο
*af**to** to kra**see** dhen **ee**-ne **kree**-o*

What liqueurs do you have?

Τι λικέρ έχετε;
*tee lee**ker** ekhe-te?*

I'll have a brandy/ a Scotch

Θα πάρω ένα μπράντυ/ουίσκι
*tha **pa**ro **e**na brandy/whisky*

A gin and tonic

Ένα τζιν και τόνικ
ena gin ke tonic

Can we hire skis here?	Μπορούμε να νοικιάσουμε σκι εδώ; *boroo-me na neekee-asoo-me skee edho?*
Could you adjust my bindings?	Μπορείτε να μου ρυθμίσετε τα λουριά; *boree-te na moo reeth-mee-se-te ta looree-a?*
A one-week ticket, please	Ένα εισιτήριο για μια βδομάδα, παρακαλώ *ena eesee-teeree-o ya meea vdhomadha para-kalo*
What are the snow conditions?	Πώς είναι το χιόνι; *pos ee-ne to khee-onee?*
Is there a restaurant at the top station?	Υπάρχει εστιατόριο στην κορυφή; *eepar-khee estee-atoree-o steen koree-fee?*
Which are the easiest runs?	Ποιες είναι οι πιο εύκολες πίστες; *pee-es ee-ne ee pee-o efko-les pees-tes?*
Is there danger of avalanches?	Υπάρχει κίνδυνος χιονοστιβάδων; *eepar-khee keen-dheenos khee-ono-steevadhon?*
Where can we go skating?	Πού μπορούμε να πάμε για πατινάζ; *poo boroo-me na pa-me ya patee-naz?*
Is there a toboggan run?	Υπάρχει ελκυθροδρόμιο; *eepar-khee elkeethro-dhromee-o?*
Can we book lessons here?	Μπορούμε να κλείσουμε μαθήματα εδώ; *boroome na kleesoome matheemata edho?*

a ένας/μία/ένα *enas/mee-a/ena*

abbey το μοναστήρι *to mona-steeree*

about: a book about Athens ένα βιβλίο για την Αθήνα *ena veevlee-o ya teen Atheena* || **at about ten o'clock** περίπου στις δέκα *pereepoo stees dheka*

above πάνω *pano*

accident το δυστύχημα *to dheestee-kheema*

accommodation η στέγη *ee ste-yee*

ache ο πόνος *o ponos*

activities οι δραστηριότητες *ee dhrasteereeotee-tes*

adaptor ο μετασχηματιστής *o meta-skheema-teestees*

address η διεύθυνση *ee dhee-ef-theensee*

adhesive tape η συγκολλητική ταινία *ee seengo-leeteekee tenee-a*

admission charge η είσοδος *ee eeso-dhos*

adult ο ενήλικος *o enee-leekos*

advance: in advance προκαταβολικώς *prokata-voleekos*

after(wards) αργότερα *argho-tera*

afternoon το απόγευμα *to apo-yevma*

aftershave το αφτερσέιβ *to aftershave*

again πάλι *palee*

ago: a week ago πριν μία βδομάδα *preen mee-a vdho-madha*

air conditioning ο κλιματισμός *o kleema-teesmos*

airline η αεροπορική εταιρία *aero-poreekee e-teree-a*

air mail αεροπορικώς *aero-poreekos*

air mattress το στρώμα για τη θάλασσα *to stroma ya tee thalasa*

airport το αεροδρόμιο *to aero-dhromee-o*

aisle *(in aircraft)* ο διάδρομος *o dheeadhromos*

alarm *(emergency)* ο συναγερμός *o seenaghermos*

alcohol το οινόπνευμα *to eeno-pnevma*

alcoholic οινοπνευματώδης *eenop-nevma-todhees*

all όλος *olos* || **all the milk** όλο το γάλα *olo to ghala* || **all (the) boys** όλα τα αγόρια *ola ta aghoree-a* || **all (the) girls** όλα τα κορίτσια *ola ta koreetsee-a*

allergic to αλλεργικός σε *aler-yeekos se*

allowance: duty-free allowance η επιτρεπόμενη ποσότητα *ee epeetrepomenee posoteeta*

all right *(agreed)* εντάξει *entaksee*

almost σχεδόν *skhedhon*

also επίσης *epeesees*

always πάντα *panda*

am see GRAMMAR

ambulance το ασθενοφόρο *to astheno-foro*

America η Αμερική *ee ameree-kee*

American Αμερικανός/ Αμερικανίδα *ameree-kanos/ ameree-kaneedha*

anaesthetic το αναισθητικό *to anes-theeteeko*

and και *ke*

another άλλος *alos* || **another glass of beer** ακόμα ένα ποτήρι μπύρα *akoma ena poteeree beera*

antibiotics τα αντιβιοτικά *ta andeeveeo-oteeka*

antifreeze το αντιπηκτικό υγρό *to andee-peekteeko eeghro*

antiseptic το αντισηπτικό *to andeeseep-teeko*

anyway οπωσδήποτε *oposdheepo-te*

anywhere οπουδήποτε *opoodheepo-te*

apartment το διαμέρισμα *to dhee-amereesma*

aperitif το απεριτίφ *to aperitif*

apple το μήλο *to meelo*

appointment το ραντεβού *to ran-devoo*

apricot το βερύκοκκο *to veree-koko*

archaeology η αρχαιολογία *ee arkheeoloyee-a*

architecture η αρχιτεκτονική *ee arkhee-tekto-neekee*

are *see* GRAMMAR

arm το μπράτσο *to bratso*

armbands *(for swimming)* τα σωσίβια χεριών *ta soseevee-a kheree-on*

around γύρω *yeero*

arrivals οι αφίξεις *ee afeeksees*

arrive φτάνω *ftano*

art gallery η πινακοθήκη *ee peenako-theekee*

artichoke η αγκινάρα *ee ankeenara*

ashtray το τασάκι *to ta-sakee*

asparagus το σπαράγγι *to spa-rangee*

aspirin η ασπιρίνη *ee aspee-reenee*

asthma το άσθμα *to asthma*

at σε *se*

aubergine η μελιτζάνα *ee meleed-zana*

Australia η Αυστραλία *ee af-stralee-a*

Australian Αυστραλός/Αυστραλίδα *af-stralos/af-straleedha*

automatic αυτόματος *afto-matos*

autumn το φθινόπωρο *to ftheeno-poro*

avalanche η χιονοστιβάδα *ee khee-onosteevadha*

avocado το αβοκάτο *to avo-kato*

baby το μωρό *to moro*

baby food οι βρεφικές τροφές *ee vrefee-kes tro-fes*

baby-sitter η μπέιμπισίτερ *ee baby sitter*

back *(of a person)* η ράχη *ee rakhee*

backpack το σακκίδιο *to sakheedhee-o*

bacon το μπαίηκον *to be-eekon*

bad *(of food)* χαλασμένος *khalas-menos* || *(of weather)* κακός *kakos*

bag *(small)* η τσάντα *ee tsanda* || *(suitcase)* η βαλίτσα *ee valeet-sa*

baggage οι αποσκευές *ee aposkeves*

baggage reclaim η αναζήτηση αποσκευών *ee ana-zeeteesee apo-skevon*

baker's ο φούρνος *o foornos*

balcony το μπαλκόνι *to balkonee*

ball η μπάλα *ee bala*

banana η μπανάνα *ee banana*

band *(musical)* η ορχήστρα *ee or-kheestra*

bandage ο επίδεσμος *o epee-dhesmos*

bank η τράπεζα ee tra-peza

bar το μπαρ to bar

barber ο κουρέας o koore-as

basket το καλάθι to kalathee

bath (tub) το μπάνιο to banee-o || to take a bath κάνω μπάνιο kano banee-o

bathing cap ο σκούφος του μπάνιου o skoofos too banee-oo

bathroom το μπάνιο to banee-o

battery η μπαταρία ee bataree-a

be see GRAMMAR

beach η πλαζ ee plaz

bean (haricot) το φασόλι to fasolee || (broad) το κουκκί to kookee || (green) το φασολάκι to faso-lakee

beautiful όμορφος omorfos

bed το κρεββάτι to kre-vatee

bedding τα κλινοσκεπάσματα ta kleeno-skepasmata

bedroom η κρεββατοκάμαρα ee krevato-kamara

beef το βοδινό to vodhee-no

beer η μπύρα ee beera

beetroot το παντζάρι to pand-zaree

before (time) πριν preen || (place) μπροστά brosta

begin αρχίζω ar-kheezo

behind πίσω peeso

below κάτω από kato apo

belt η ζώνη ee zonee

beside δίπλα σε dheepla se

best ο καλύτερος o kalee-teros

better (than) καλύτερος (από) kalee-teros (apo)

between μεταξύ metak-see

bicycle το ποδήλατο to podheela-to

big μεγάλος meghalos

bigger μεγαλύτερος meghaleeteros

bikini το μπικίνι to beekeenee

bill ο λογαριασμός o logharee-asmos

bin ο κάλαθος των αχρήστων o kala-thos ton akhree-ston

binoculars τα κιάλια ta kee-alee-a

bird το πουλί to poolee

birthday τα γενέθλια ta yenethlee-a || happy birthday! ευτυχισμένα γενέθλια eftee-khees-mena yenethlee-a

birthday card η κάρτα γενεθλίων ee karta yenethlee-on

bit: a bit (of) ένα κομμάτι ena komatee

bitten: I have been bitten με δάγκωσε me dhangose

bitter πικρός peekros

black μαύρος mavros

blackcurrant το μαύρο φραγκοστάφυλο to mavro frango-stafeelo

blanket η κουβέρτα ee koo-verta

bleach το λευκαντικό to lefkan-deeko

blocked (pipe) βουλωμένος voolo-menos || (nose) κλειστή kleestee

blood group η ομάδα αίματος ee omadha ematos

blouse η μπλούζα ee blooza

blow-dry στέγνωμα stegh-noma

blue γαλάζιος ghalazee-os

boarding card το δελτίο επιβιβάσεως to dheltee-o epee-veevase-os

boarding house η πανσιόν ee panseeon

boat *(small)* η βάρκα *ee varka* ‖ *(ship)* το πλοίο *to plee-o*

boat trip η βαρκάδα *ee varkadha*

book[1] *n* το βιβλίο *to veevlee-o*

book[2] *vb (room, tickets)* κλείνω *kleeno*

booking: to make a booking κλείνω θέση *kleeno thesee*

booking office *(railways, airlines)* το εκδοτήριο *to ekdhoteeree-o* ‖ *(theatre)* το ταμείο *to tamee-o*

bookshop το βιβλιοπωλείο *to veevlee-opolee-o*

boots οι μπότες *ee botes*

border *(frontier)* τα σύνορα *ta seen-ora*

both και οι δυο *ke ee dhee-o*

bottle το μπουκάλι *to boo-kalee*

bottle-opener το ανοιχτήρι *to aneekhteeree*

box *(container)* το κιβώτιο *to keevotee-o* ‖ *(cardboard)* το κουτί *to kootee*

box office το ταμείο *to tamee-o*

boy το αγόρι *to agho-ree*

boyfriend ο φίλος *o feelos*

bra το σουτιέν *to sootee-en*

bracelet το βραχιόλι *to vrakhee-olee*

brake fluid το υγρό των φρένων *to eeghro ton frenon*

brakes τα φρένα *ta frena*

brandy το κονιάκ *to konee-ak*

bread το ψωμί *to psomee*

breakable εύθραυστος *ef-thrav-stos*

breakdown η βλάβη *ee vlavee*

breakdown van το συνεργείο διασώσεως *to seeneryee-o dhee-aso-se-os*

breakfast το πρόγευμα *to pro-yevma*

breast το στήθος *to steethos*

briefcase ο χαρτοφύλακας *o kharto-feelakas*

bring φέρνω *ferno*

Britain η Βρετανία *ee vretanee-a*

British Βρετανός/Βρετανίδα *vreta-nos/vretaneedha*

brochure η μπροσούρα *ee brosoora*

broken σπασμένος *spas-menos* ‖ **broken down** χαλασμένος *khalas-menos*

brooch η καρφίτσα *ee karfeet-sa*

broom η σκούπα *ee skoopa*

brother ο αδελφός *o adhel-fos*

brown καφέ *kafe*

brush η βούρτσα *ee voort-sa*

bucket ο κουβάς *o koovas*

buffet ο μπουφές *o boo-fes*

buffet car το βαγκόν ρεστωράν *to vankon restoran*

bulb *(light)* η λάμπα *ee lampa*

bureau de change *(bank)* ξένο συνάλλαγμα *kseno seenalaghma*

burnt καμένος *ka-menos*

burst σκάζω *ska-zo*

bus το λεωφορείο *to leo-foree-o*

business η δουλειά *ee dhoolee-a*

bus station ο σταθμός του λεωφορείου *o stath-mos too leo-foree-oo*

bus stop η στάση του λεωφορείου *ee stasee too leo-foree-oo*

bus tour η εκδρομή με λεωφορείο *ee ek-dhromee me leo-foree-o*

busy απασχολημένος *apas-kholee-menos*

but αλλά *ala*

butcher's το κρεοπωλείο *to kreo polee-o*

butter ο βούτυρος *o voo-teeros*

button το κουμπί *to koombee*

buy αγοράζω *agho-razo*

by *(beside)* κοντά σε *konda se* || *(time)* μέχρι *mekhree*

bypass ο παρακαμπτήριος *o parakamteeree-os*

cabaret το καμπαρέ *to kabare*

cabbage το λάχανο *to lakhano*

cable car ο κρεμαστός σιδηρόδρομος *o krema-stos seedheero-dhromos*

café το καφενείο *to ka-fenee-o*

cake το γλύκισμα *to ghlee-keesma*

call[1] *vb* φωνάζω *fonazo*

call[2] *n* *(telephone)* η κλήση *ee kleesee* || **a long-distance call** υπεραστική κλήση *eeperasteekee kleesee*

calm ήσυχος *eesee-khos*

camera η φωτογραφική μηχανή *ee foto-ghrafeekee meekha-nee*

camp κατασκηνώνω *kata-skeenono*

camp site χώρος κατασκηνώσεως *khoros kata-skeeno-se-os*

can[1] *vb* : **I can** μπορώ *boro* || **you can** μπορείς *borees* || **he can** μπορεί *boree*

can[2] *n* *(of food)* η κονσέρβα *ee kon-serva* || *(for oil)* ο τενεκές *o te-ne-kes*

Canada ο Καναδάς *o kana-dhas*

Canadian Καναδός/Καναδή *Kana-dhos/Kanadhee*

cancel ακυρώνω *akee-rono*

canoe το κανό *to kano*

can-opener το ανοιχτήρι *to aneekh-teeree*

car το αυτοκίνητο *to afto-keeneeto*

carafe η καράφα *ee karafa*

caravan το τροχόσπιτο *to trokho-speeto*

carburettor το καρμπιρατέρ *to karbee-rater*

card η κάρτα *ee karta*

cardigan το πλεκτό *to plekto*

careful προσεκτικός *prosek-teekhos*

car ferry το φέρρυμπωτ *to fereebot*

car park το πάρκινγκ *to parkeeng*

carpet το χαλί *to khalee* || *(fitted)* η μοκέτα *ee mo-keta*

carriage *(railway)* το βαγόνι *to vaghonee* || *(transport of goods)* η μεταφορά *ee meta-fora*

carrot το καρότο *to karoto*

carry κουβαλώ *koo-valo*

car wash το πλύσιμο αυτοκινήτων *to plee-seemo afto-keeneeton*

case η υπόθεση *ee eepo-thesee* || *(suitcase)* η βαλίτσα *ee valeet-sa*

cash[1] *vb* *(cheque)* εξαργυρώνω *eksar-yeerono*

cash[2] *n* τα μετρητά *ta metree-ta*

cash desk το ταμείο *to tamee-o*

cashier ο ταμίας *o tamee-as*

casino το καζίνο *to kazeeno*

cassette η κασέτα *ee ka-seta*

castle το κάστρο *to kastro*

catch πιάνω *pee-ano*

cathedral ο καθεδρικός ναός *o kathedh-reekos naos*

Catholic καθολικός *katho-likos*

cauliflower το κουνουπίδι *to*

koonoo-peedhee

cave η σπηλιά *ee speelee-a*

celery το σέλινο *to seleeno*

cemetery το νεκροταφείο *to nekro-tafee-o*

centimetre ο πόντος *o pondos*

central κεντρικός *kendree-kos*

centre το κέντρο *to kendro*

cereal (for breakfast) το σήριαλ *to seeree-al*

certain βέβαιος *ve-ve-os*

certificate το πιστοποιητικό *to peestopee-eeteeko*

chain η αλυσίδα *ee alee-seedha*

chair η καρέκλα *ee karekla*

chair lift η κρεμαστή καρέκλα *ee kremastee karekla*

champagne η σαμπάνια *ee sambanee-a*

change¹ n η αλλαγή *ee ala-yee* || (money) τα ρέστα *ta resta*

change² vb αλλάζω *alazo*

changing room (beach, sports) το αποδυτήριο *to apodhee-teeree-o*

chapel το παρεκκλήσι *to parek-leesee*

charge η τιμή *ee teemee*

charter flight η ναυλωμένη πτήση *ee navlo-menee pteesee*

cheap φτηνός *fteenos*

cheaper φτηνότερος *fteeno-teros*

check ελέγχω *elen-kho*

check in να είμαι στο αεροδρόμιο *na ee-me sto aero-dhromee-o*

check-in desk ο έλεγχος εισιτηρίων *o elen-khos eesee-teeree-on*

cheerio! γεια *ya*

cheers! (your health) στην υγειά σας *steen ee-ya sas*

cheese το τυρί *to teeree*

chemist's το φαρμακείο *to farmakee-o*

cheque η επιταγή *ee epee-tayee*

cheque book το βιβλιαράκι επιταγών *to veevlee-arakee epee-taghon*

cherry το κεράσι *to kerasee*

chestnut το κάστανο *to kastano*

chewing gum η τσίχλα *ee tseekh-la*

chicken το κοτόπουλο *to koto-poolo*

chickenpox η ανεμοβλογιά *ee anemovlogheea*

child το παιδί *to pedhee*

children τα παιδιά *ta pedhee-a*

chilli η κοκκινοπιπεριά *ee kokeeno-peeperee-a*

chilled: is the wine chilled? είναι κρύο το κρασί; *ee-ne kree-o to krasee?*

chips πατάτες τηγανιτές *pata-tes teeghanee-tes*

chocolate η σοκολάτα *ee soko-lata*

chocolates οι σοκολάτες *ee sokolates*

Christmas τα Χριστούγεννα *ta khreestoo-yena* || **merry Christmas!** καλά Χριστούγεννα *kala khree-stoo-yena*

church η εκκλησία *ee ekleesee-a*

cider ο μηλίτης *o meeleetees*

cigar το πούρο *to pooro*

cigarette το τσιγάρο *to tsee-gharo*

cigarette paper το τσιγαρόχαρτο *to tsigharokharto*

cinema ο κινηματογράφος *o keeneema-toghrafos*

circus το τσίρκο *to tseerko*

city η πόλη *ee polee*

clean¹ *adj* καθαρός *katha-ros*

clean² *vb* καθαρίζω *katha-reezo*

cleansing cream η κρέμα καθαρισμού *ee krema katha-reesmoo*

client ο πελάτης/η πελάτισσα *o pela-tees/ee pelateesa*

climbing η ορειβασία *ee oree-vasee-a*

climbing boots οι μπότες ορειβασίας *ee bo-tes oree-vasee-as*

cloakroom η γκαρνταρόμπα *ee garda-roba*

clock το ρολόι *to rolo-ee*

close¹ *vb* κλείνω *kleeno*

close² *adj (near)* κοντινός *kondee-nos* || *(weather)* αποπνιχτικός *apopneekh-teekos*

closed κλειστός *kleestos*

cloth το πανί *to panee* || *(for floor)* το σφουγγαρόπανο *to sfoonga-ropano*

clothes τα ρούχα *ta rookha*

clothes peg το μανταλάκι *to manda-lakhee*

cloudy συννεφιασμένος *seenefee-asmenos*

cloves τα γαρύφαλλα *ta gharee-fala*

club η λέσχη *ee leskhee*

coach *(railway)* το βαγόνι *to vaghonee* || *(bus)* το πούλμαν *to poolman* || *(instructor)* ο προπονητής *o propo-neetees*

coach trip το ταξίδι με πούλμαν *to tak-seedhee me poolman*

coast οι ακτές *ee ak-tes*

coastguard η ακτοφυλακή *ee akto-feelakee*

coat το παλτό *to palto*

coat hanger η κρεμάστρα *ee krema-stra*

cocktail το κοκτέιλ *to kokte-eel*

cocoa το κακάο *to kaka-o*

coconut η καρύδα *ee kareedha*

coffee ο καφές *o ka-fes* || **black coffee** σκέτος καφές *sketos kafes* || **white coffee** καφές με γάλα *kafes me ghala*

coin το νόμισμα *to nomees-ma*

cold κρύος *kree-os* || **I have a cold** είμαι κρυωμένος *ee-me kree-o-menos* || **I'm cold** κρυώνω *kree-ono*

colour το χρώμα *to khroma*

colour film το έγχρωμο φιλμ *to en-khromo feelm*

comb η χτένα *ee khtena*

come έρχομαι *erkho-me* || **to come back** γυρίζω *yee-reezo* || **to come in** μπαίνω *beno*

comfortable αναπαυτικός *anapaf-teekos*

communion *(holy)* η θεία κοινωνία *ee thee-a keenoneea*

company *(firm)* η εταιρία *ee e-teree-a*

compartment το διαμέρισμα *to dhee-a-mereesma*

complain παραπονούμαι *para-ponoo-me*

compulsory υποχρεωτικός *eepokhre-oteekos*

computer το κομπιούτερ *to kompee-ooter*

concert η συναυλία *ee seenavlee-a*

condensed milk συμπυκνωμένο

γάλα *seembeeknomeno ghala*

condition η κατάσταση *ee kata-stasee*

conditioner το κοντίσιονερ *to kondeesee-oner*

conductor (in bus or train) ο εισπράκτορας *o ees-praktoras*

conference η διάσκεψη *ee dheeaskepsee*

confession (religious) η εξομολόγηση *ee eksomolo-yeesee*

confirm επιβεβαιώνω *epee-veve-ono*

congratulations! συγχαρητήρια *seenkharee-teeree-a*

connection (trains, etc) η σύνδεση *ee seen-dhesee*

constipated: to be constipated έχω δυσκοιλιότητα *e-kho dheeskeelee-oteeta*

consulate το προξενείο *to proksenee-o*

contact επικοινωνώ *epeekee-nono*

contact lenses οι φακοί επαφής *ee fakee epa-fees*

contact lens cleaner το υγρό καθαρισμού *to eeghro kathareesmoo*

Continental breakfast το ευρωπαϊκό πρόγευμα *to evropa-eeko pro-yevma*

contraceptives τα αντισυλληπτικά *ta andeesee-leepteeka*

cook μαγειρεύω *mayee-revo*

cooker η κουζίνα *ee koo-zeena*

cool δροσερός *dhro-seros*

copy[1] vb αντιγράφω *andeeghrafo*

copy[2] n το αντίγραφο *to andee-ghrafo*

corkscrew το τιρμπουσόν *to teer-booson*

corn (sweet corn) το καλαμπόκι *to kalam-bokee* || **corn on the cob** ο αραβόσιτος *o aravo-seetos*

corner η γωνία *ee ghonee-a*

cornflakes τα κορνφλέικς *ta cornflakes*

cortisone η κορτιζόνη *ee korteezonee*

cosmetics τα καλλυντικά *ta kaleen-deeka*

cost στοιχίζω *stee-kheezo*

cotton το βαμβάκι *to vamvakee*

cotton wool το βαμβάκι *to vam-vakee*

couchette η κουκέτα *ee koo-keta*

cough ο βήχας *o veekhas*

country η χώρα *ee khora* || (not town) η εξοχή *ee ek-sokhee*

couple το ζευγάρι *to zev-gharee*

courgette το κολοκυθάκι *to kolokee-thakee*

courier (for tourists) ο/η συνοδός *o/ee seen-odhos*

course (meal) το πιάτο *to pee-ato*

cousin ο εξάδελφος/η εξαδέλφη *o eksa-dhelfos/ee eksa-dhelfee*

crab το καβούρι *to ka-vooree*

crash η σύγκρουση *ee seenkroosee*

crash helmet το προστατευτικό κράνος *to prosta-tefteeko kranos*

cream η κρέμα *ee krema*

credit card η πιστωτική κάρτα *ee peesto-teekee karta*

crisps οι πατατίτσες *ee patateetses*

croquette η κροκέτα *ee kro-keta*

cross περνώ απέναντι *perno apenandee*

crossroads το σταυροδρόμι *to stavro-dhromee*

crowded γεμάτος *yematos*

cruise η κρουαζιέρα *ee kroo-azee-era*

cucumber το αγγούρι *to angooree*

cup το φλιτζάνι *to fleed-zanee*

cupboard το ντουλάπι *to doo-lapee*

currant η σταφίδα *ee sta-feedha*

current *(electric)* το ρεύμα *to revma*

cushion το μαξιλάρι *to maksee-laree*

custard η κρέμα *ee krema*

customs το τελωνείο *to telonee-o*

cut[1] *vb* κόβω *kovo*

cut[2] *n* το κόψιμο *to kop-seemo*

cutlery τα μαχαιροπήρουνα *ta makhero-peeroona*

cycle το ποδήλατο *to podhee-lato*

cycling η ποδηλασία *ee podhee-lasee-a*

daily ημερήσιος *eemereesee-os*

damage η ζημιά *ee zeemee-a*

damp υγρός *eeghros*

dance[1] *n* ο χορός *o khoros*

dance[2] *vb* χορεύω *kho-revo*

dangerous επικίνδυνος *epee-keendheenos*

dark *(colour)* σκούρο *skooro* || *it's dark* είναι σκοτεινά *ee-ne skotee-na*

date η ημερομηνία *ee eemero-meenee-a* || *what's the date?* τι ημερομηνία είναι; *tee eemero-meenee-a ee-ne?* || *date of birth* η ημερομηνία γεννήσεως *ee eemero-meenee-a yeneesee-os*

daughter η κόρη *ee koree*

day η μέρα *ee mera*

dear αγαπητός *agha-peetos* || *(expensive)* ακριβός *akree-vos*

decaffeinated χωρίς καφείνη *khorees kafe-eenee*

deck chair η σαιζλόγκ *ee sez-long*

declare δηλώνω *dhee-lono*

deep βαθύς *vathees*

deep freeze η κατάψυξη *ee katapseeksee*

defrost *(windscreen, food)* ξεπαγώνω *ksepa-ghono*

de-ice αποπαγώνω *apopaghono*

delay η καθυστέρηση *ee kathee-stereesee*

delicious νόστιμος *no-steemos*

dentist ο/η οδοντογιατρός *o/ee odhonto-yatros*

dentures η οδοντοστοιχία *ee odhonto-steekhee-a*

deodorant το αποσμητικό *to apos-meeteeko*

department store το πολυκατάστημα *to poleeka-tasteema*

departure η αναχώρηση *ee ana-khoreesee* || **departure lounge** η αίθουσα αναχωρήσεων *ee ethoo-sa ana-khoreesee-on*

deposit *(in a bank)* η κατάθεση *ee kata-thesee* || *(part payment)* η προκαταβολή *ee proka-tavolee*

dessert το επιδόρπιο *to epee-dhorpee-o*

details οι λεπτομέρειες *ee lepto-meree-es*

detergent το απορρυπαντικό *to aporee-panteeko*

detour: to make a detour βγαίνω από το δρόμο *vgheno apo to dhromo*

develop αναπτύσσω *anap-teeso*

diabetic διαβητικός *dhee-avee-teekos*

dialling code ο τηλεφωνικός κώδικας *o teele-foneekos kodhee-kas*

diamond το διαμάντι *to dhee-amandee*

diarrhoea η διάρροια *ee dhee-aree-a*

diary το ημερολόγιο *to eemero-loyee-o*

dictionary το λεξικό *to leksee-ko*

diesel το ντίζελ *to deezel*

diet η δίαιτα *ee dhee-eta*

different διαφορετικός *dhee-afore-teekos*

difficult δύσκολος *dhees-kolos*

dinghy η λαστιχένια βάρκα *ee lasteekhenee-a varka*

dining room η τραπεζαρία *ee trapezaree-a*

dinner το δείπνο *to dheepno*

direct άμεσος *a-mesos*

directory *(telephone)* ο τηλεφωνικός κατάλογος *o teele-foneekos kata-loghos*

dirty ακάθαρτος *aka-thartos*

disabled ανάπηρος *ana-peeros*

disco η δισκοθήκη *ee dheeskotheekee*

discount η έκπτωση *ee ek-ptosee*

dish το πιάτο *to pee-ato*

dishtowel το ποτηρόπανο *to poteeropano*

dishwasher το πλυντήριο πιάτων *to pleenteeree-o pee-aton*

disinfectant το απολυμαντικό *to apolee-mandeeko*

distilled water το απεσταγμένο νερό *to apestagh-meno nero*

divorced ο ζωντοχήρος/η ζωντοχήρα *o zondo-kheeros/ee zondo-kheera*

dizzy ζαλισμένος *zalees-menos*

do: I do κάνω *kano* || **you do** κάνεις *kanees*

doctor ο/η γιατρός *o/ee yatros*

documents τα έγγραφα *ta en-grafa*

doll η κούκλα *ee kookla*

dollar το δολλάριο *to dholaree-o*

door η πόρτα *ee porta*

double διπλός *dheeplos*

double bed το διπλό κρεββάτι *to dheeplo kre-vatee*

double room το δίκλινο δωμάτιο *to dhee-kleeno dhomatee-o*

down: to go down κατεβαίνω *kate-veno*

downstairs κάτω *kato*

drachmas δραχμές *dhrakh-mes*

draught *(in room)* το ρεύμα *to revma*

dress[1] *n* το φόρεμα *to fore-ma*

dress[2] *vb* ντύνομαι *deeno-me*

dressing *(for salad)* το λαδολέμονο *to ladho-lemono*

drink[1] *n* το ποτό *to poto* || **have a drink** παίρνω ένα ποτό *perno ena poto*

drink[2] *vb* πίνω *peeno*

drinking chocolate η σοκολάτα *ee sokolata*

drinking water το πόσιμο νερό *to poseemo nero*

drive οδηγώ *odhee-gho*

driver ο οδηγός *o odhee-ghos*

driving licence η άδεια οδήγησης *ee adhee-a odhee-yeesees*

drunk μεθυσμένος *methees-menos*

dry[1] adj στεγνός *stegh-nos*

dry[2] vb στεγνώνω *stegh-nono*

dry-cleaner's το καθαριστήριο *to katharee-steeree-o*

duck η πάπια *ee papee-a*

due: when is the train due? πότε θα φθάσει το τραίνο; *po-te tha fthasee to treno*

dummy η πιπίλα *ee pee-peela*

during κατά τη διάρκεια *kata tee dhee-arkee-a*

duty-free αφορολόγητος *afo-rolo-yeetos*

duty-free shop κατάστημα αφορολόγητων *kata-steema afo-rolo-yeeton*

duvet το πάπλωμα *to paplo-ma*

dynamo το δυναμό *to dheena-mo*

each κάθε *ka-the* || **100 drachmas each** εκατό δραχμές ο καθένας *ekato drakh-mes o ka-thenas*

ear το αυτί *to aftee*

earache: I have earache με πονάει το αυτί μου *me pona-ee to aftee moo*

earlier νωρίτερα *noree-tera*

early νωρίς *norees*

earrings τα σκουλαρίκια *ta skoola-reekee-a*

east η ανατολή *ee ana-tolee*

Easter το Πάσχα *to paskha*

easy εύκολος *ef-kolos*

eat τρώω *tro-o*

eel το χέλι *to khelee*

egg το αυγό *to av-gho* || **fried eggs** αυγά τηγανητά *avgha teeghaneeta* || **boiled eggs** αυγά βραστά *avgha vrasta* || **poached eggs** αυγά ποσέ *avgha pose* || **egg cup** η αυγοθήκη *ee avgho-theekee*

either … or η … ή/είτε … είτε *ee …ee/eete … eete*

elastic το λάστιχο *to la-steekho*

elastic band το λαστιχάκι *to lastee-khakee*

electric ηλεκτρικός *eelek-treekhos*

electrician ο ηλεκτρολόγος *o eelektro-loghos*

electricity ο ηλεκτρισμός *o eelek-treesmos*

electricity meter ο μετρητής ηλεκτρισμού *o metree-tees eelek-treesmoo*

electric razor ηλεκτρική ξυριστική μηχανή *eelektreekee kseereesteekee meekhanee*

embassy η πρεσβεία *ee presvee-a*

emergency: it's an emergency είναι κρίσιμη περίσταση *ee-ne kree-seemee peree-stasee*

empty άδειος *adhee-os*

end το τέλος *to telos*

engaged (to be married) αρραβωνιασμένος/η *aravonee-asmenos/nee* || (toilet) κατειλημένη *kateelee-menee* || (phone) μιλάει *meelaee*

engine η μηχανή *ee mee-khanee*

England η Αγγλία *ee anglee-a*

English Άγγλος/Αγγλίδα *anglos/angleedha*

enjoy: to enjoy oneself διασκεδάζω *dhee-aske-dhazo*

enough αρκετά *arke-ta* || **enough bread** αρκετό ψωμί *arke-to psomee*

enquiry desk/office γραφείο πληροφοριών *ghrafee-o pleero-foree-on*

entertainment η ψυχαγωγία *ee pseekha-ghoyee-a*

entrance η είσοδος *ee eesodhos*

entrance fee η είσοδος *ee eesodhos*

envelope ο φάκελλος *o fa-kelos*

equipment ο εξοπλισμός *o eksoplees-mos*

escalator η κυλιόμενη σκάλα *ee keelee-omenee skala*

especially ειδικά *eedhee-ka*

essential απαραίτητος *apare-teetos*

Eurocheque η ευρωεπιταγή *ee evro-epeetaghee*

Europe η Ευρώπη *ee evropee*

evening το βράδυ *to vradhee* || **this evening** απόψε *apop-se* || **in the evening** το βράδυ *to vradhee*

every κάθε *ka-the*

everyone όλοι *olee*

everything όλα *ola*

excellent εξαιρετικός *ekse-reteekos*

except εκτός από *ektos apo*

excess luggage επί πλέον αποσκευές *epee pleon apo-skeves*

exchange[1] *vb* ανταλλάζω *anda-lazo*

exchange[2] *n* η ανταλλαγή *ee anda-layee*

exchange rate η τιμή του συναλλάγματος *ee teemee too seenalagh-matos*

excursion η εκδρομή *ee ek-dhromee*

excuse me με συγχωρείτε *me seenkho-reete*

exhaust pipe η εξάτμιση *ee eksat-meesee*

exhibition η έκθεση *ee ek-thesee*

exit η έξοδος *ee ekso-dhos*

expensive ακριβός *akree-vos*

expert ο/η ειδικός *o/ee eedhee-kos*

expire λήγω *leegho*

express *(train)* η ταχεία *ee takhee-a*

express letter το κατεπείγον γράμμα *to ka-te-peeghon ghrama*

extra: it costs extra στοιχίζει επιπλέον *stee-kheezee epee-ple-on* || **extra money** περισσότερα χρήματα *peree-sotera khree-mata*

eyeliner αϊλάινερ *eye-liner*

eyes τα μάτια *ta matee-a*

eye shadow σκιά για τα μάτια *skeea ya ta mateea*

face το πρόσωπο *to pro-sopo*

facilities οι ευκολίες *ee ef-kolee-es*

faint λιποθυμώ *leepo-theemo*

fainted λιποθύμησε *leepo-theemeese*

fair[1] *adj (hair)* ξανθός *ksanthos*

fair[2] *n (commercial)* η έκθεση *ee ek-thesee* || *(fun fair)* το λούνα παρκ *to loona park*

fall πέφτω *pefto*

family η οικογένεια *ee eeko-yenee-a*

famous διάσημος *dhee-aseemos*

fan (electric) ο ανεμιστήρας *o anemee-stee*ras || (supporter) ο θαυμαστής/η θαυμάστρια *o thav-mastees/ee thav-mastree-a*

fan belt η ταινία του ανεμιστήρα *ee tenee-a too a-nemees-tee*ra

far μακριά *makree-a*

fare (in bus, train) τα ναύλα *ta nav*la

farm το αγρόκτημα *to aghrok-teema*

fast γρήγορα *ghree-ghora*

fat[1] adj χοντρός *khond*ros

fat[2] n το λίπος *to lee*pos

father ο πατέρας *o pa-te*ras

fault: it was not my fault δε φταίω εγώ *dhe fte-o egho*

favourite ο πιο αγαπημένος *o pee-o agha-pee*menos

feed τρέφω *tre*fo || (baby) ταΐζω *ta-eezo*

feel (with hand, etc) ψηλαφώ *pseela-fo* || I feel sick θέλω να κάνω εμετό *thelo na kano eme-to*

ferry το φέρρυμπωτ *to feree-bot*

festival το φεστιβάλ *to festeeval*

fetch φέρνω *ferno*

fever ο πυρετός *o peere*tos

few: a few μερικοί *meree-kee*

fiancé(e) ο μνηστήρας/η μνηστή *o mnee-stee*ras/*ee mnees*tee

field το χωράφι *to kho-ra*fee

fill γεμίζω *ye-mee*zo || to fill up γεμίζω *ye-mee*zo || fill it up! (car) γεμίστε το *ye-mees-te to*

fillet το φιλέτο *to fee*leto

filling (in cake, etc) το γέμισμα *to yemees-ma* || (in tooth) το σφράγισμα *to sfra-yeesma*

film (for camera) το φιλμ *to film* ||

(in cinema) η ταινία *ee te*nee-a

filter το φίλτρο *to fee*ltro

filter-tipped με φίλτρο *me fee*ltro

finish τελειώνω *tele-ono*

fire (heater) η θερμάστρα *ee thermas-tra* || fire! φωτιά! *fotee-a!* || fire brigade η πυροσβεστική *ee peeros-vesteekee* || fire extinguisher ο πυροσβεστήρας *o peeros-veste*ras

fireworks τα πυροτεχνήματα *ta peerotekh-nee*mata

first πρώτος *pro*tos

first aid οι πρώτες βοήθειες *ee pro-tes vo-ee*thee-es

first class (seat, etc) η πρώτη θέση *ee pro*tee *the*see

first floor το πρώτο πάτωμα *to proto pa*toma

first name το όνομα *to o*noma

fish[1] n το ψάρι *to psa*ree

fish[2] vb ψαρεύω *psa-re*vo

fit (healthy) υγιής *eeyee-ees*

fix επιδιορθώνω *epeedhee-ortho*no || (arrange) κανονίζω *kano-nee*zo

fizzy (drink) αεριούχο *aeree-oo*kho

flash (on camera) το φλας *to flas*

flask ο θέρμος *o ther*mos

flat (apartment) το διαμέρισμα *to dhee-ame*reesma

flat tyre: I have a flat tyre μ' έχει πιάσει λάστιχο *mekhee pee*asee *lasteekho*

flight η πτήση *ee ptee*see

flippers τα πτερύγια *ta ptereeyee-a*

floor το πάτωμα *to pa*toma || (storey) ο όροφος *o o*rofos

flour το αλεύρι *to alev-ree*

flower το λουλούδι *to loo-loodhee*

flu η γρίππη *ee ghreepee*

fly η μύγα *ee meegha*

fog η ομίχλη *ee omeekhlee*

follow ακολουθώ *ako-lootho*

food το φαγητό *to fa-yeeto*

food poisoning η τροφική δηλητηρίαση *ee trofee-kee dheelee-teeree-asee*

foot το πόδι *to podhee* || *(measure)* see **CONVERSION CHARTS**

football το ποδόσφαιρο *to podhos-fero*

for για *ya*

foreign ξένος *ksenos*

forest το δάσος *to dhasos*

forget ξεχνώ *ksekh-no*

fork το πηρούνι *to pee-roonee* || *(in road)* η διακλάδωση *ee thee-akladhosee*

fortnight το δεκαπενθήμερο *to dhekapen-theemero*

fountain το σιντριβάνι *to seendree-vanee*

free ελεύθερος *elef-theros* || *(costing nothing)* δωρεάν *dho-re-an*

freezer ο καταψύκτης *o katap-seektees*

French γαλλικός *ghaleekos*

French beans τα φασολάκια *ta faso-lakee-a*

frequent συχνός *seekh-nos*

fresh φρέσκος *freskos*

fridge το ψυγείο *to psee-yee-o*

fried τηγανητός *teegha-neetos*

friend ο φίλος/η φίλη *o feelos/ee feelee*

from από *apo*

front *(part)* το μπροστινό (μέρος) *to brostee-no (meros)* || **in front** μπροστά *brosta*

frosty ψυχρός *pseechros*

frozen *(water)* παγωμένος *pagho-menos* || *(food)* κατεψυγμένος *katep-seegh-menos*

fruit τα φρούτα *ta froota*

fruit juice ο χυμός φρούτων *o kheemos frooton*

fruit salad η φρουτοσαλάτα *ee frooto-salata*

frying pan το τηγάνι *to tee-ghanee*

fuel τα καύσιμα *ta kaf-seema*

fuel pump η αντλία καυσίμων *ee andlee-a kaf-seemon*

full γεμάτος *ye-matos*

full board (η) πλήρης διατροφή *(ee) pleerees dhee-atrofee*

funny αστείος *astee-os*

fur η γούνα *ee ghoona*

fuse η ασφάλεια *ee asfalee-a*

gallery *(art)* η πινακοθήκη *ee peenako-theekee*

gallon see **CONVERSION CHARTS**

gambling η χαρτοπαιξία *ee kharto-peksee-a*

game το παιγνίδι *to pegh-needhee* || *(to eat)* το κυνήγι *to keenee-yee*

garage το γκαράζ *to garaz*

garden ο κήπος *o keepos*

garlic το σκόρδο *to skordho*

gas το γκάζι *to gazee*

gas cylinder η φιάλη γκαζιού *ee fee-alee gazee-oo*

gears οι ταχύτητες *ee takheeteetes*

gentleman ο κύριος *o keeree-os*

Gents' Ανδρών *andhron*

genuine γνήσιος *ghnee*see-os

germ το μικρόβιο *to* meek*rovee-o*

German measles η ερυθρά *ee ereeth*ra

get αποκτώ *apok-to* || **to get in** (car, etc) μπαίνω *beno* || **to get off** (from bus) κατεβαίνω *ka-te-veno* || **to get on a bus** ανεβαίνω στο λεωφορείο *a-ne-veno sto leo-foree-o* || **to get through** (on the phone) συνδέομαι *seen-dhe-o-me*

gift το δώρο *to dhoro*

gift shop νεωτερισμοί *neoteree*smee

gin το τζιν *to dzeen*

ginger η πιπερόρριζα *ee peepero-reeza*

girl το κορίτσι *to koreet-see*

girlfriend η φίλη *ee feelee*

give δίνω *dheeno*

glass (to drink from) το ποτήρι *to poteeree*

glasses (spectacles) τα γυαλιά *to yalee-a*

gloves τα γάντια *ta ghandee-a*

glucose η γλυκόζη *ee ghleekozee*

glue¹ n η κόλλα *ee kola*

glue² vb κολλώ *kolo*

go πηγαίνω *pee-yeno* || **I go/I am going** πηγαίνω *pee-yeno* || **you go/you are going** πηγαίνεις *pee-yenees* || **to go down** κατεβαίνω *ka-te-veno* || **to go in** μπαίνω *beno* || **to go out** βγαίνω *vgheno* || **to go up** ανεβαίνω *a-ne-veno*

goat η κατσίκα *ee kat-seeka*

goggles (for swimming, etc) τα προστατευτικά γυαλιά *ta prosta-tefteeka yalee-a*

gold ο χρυσός *o khree*sos || (made of gold) χρυσός *khree*sos

golf το γκολφ *to golf*

golf course το γήπεδο του γκολφ *to yee-pedho too golf*

good καλός *kalos*

good afternoon χαίρετε *khe-re-te*

goodbye αντίο *andee-o*

good day καλημέρα *kalee-mera*

good evening καλησπέρα *kalee-spera*

good morning καλημέρα *kalee-mera*

good night καληνύκτα *kalee-neekhta*

goose η χήνα *ee kheena*

gramme το γραμμάριο *to ghramaree-o*

grandfather ο παππούς *o papoos*

grandmother η γιαγιά *ee ya-ya*

grapefruit το γκρέιπ-φρουτ *to grapefruit*

grapefruit juice ο χυμός γκρέιπ-φρουτ *o kheemos grapefruit*

grapes τα σταφύλια *ta stafeelee-a*

grass το γρασίδι *to ghra-seedhee*

greasy λιπαρός *lee-paros*

great μεγάλος *me-ghalos*

Greece η Ελλάδα *ee eladha*

greedy λαίμαργος *lemar-ghos*

Greek¹ n 'Ελληνας/Ελληνίδα *elee-nas/elee-needha*

Greek² adj ελληνικός *elleeneekos*

green πράσινος *prasee-nos*

green card η πράσινη κάρτα *ee prasee-nee karta*

grey γκρίζος *gree*zos

grilled της σχάρας *tees skharas*

grocer's το μπακάλικο *to baka-leeko*

ground[1] *n* το έδαφος *to edha-fos*

ground[2] *adj (coffee, etc)* αλεσμένος *ales-menos*

ground floor το ισόγειο *to eeso-yee-o*

groundsheet ο μουσαμάς εδάφους *o moosamas edhafoos*

group η ομάδα *ee omadha*

group passport ομαδικό διαβατήριο *omadheeko dhee-avateerio*

grow μεγαλώνω *megha-lono*

guarantee η εγγύηση *ee engee-eesee*

guard *(in train)* ο υπεύθυνος τραίνου *o eepef-theenos trenoo*

guest ο φιλοξενούμενος *o feelok-senoo-menos*

guesthouse ο ξενώνας *o kse-nonas*

guide[1] *n* ο/η ξεναγός *o/ee ksena-ghos*

guide[2] *vb* ξεναγώ *ksenagho*

guidebook ο οδηγός *o odhee-ghos*

guided tour η περιήγηση με ξεναγό *ee peree-eeyeesee me ksena-gho*

gym shoes τα παπούτσια γυμναστικής *ta papootsee-a yeemna-steekees*

haemorrhoids οι αιμορροΐδες *ee emoroeedhes*

hair τα μαλλιά *ta malee-a*

hairbrush η βούρτσα *ee voortsa*

haircut το κούρεμα *to koo-rema*

hairdresser ο κομμωτής/η κομμώτρια *o komo-tees/ee komotree-a*

hair dryer ο στεγνωτήρας *o steghno-teeras*

hairgrip το τσιμπιδάκι *to tseembee-dhakee*

hair spray το σπρέι για μαλλιά *to spre-ee ya malee-a*

half το μισό *to meeso* || **half an hour** μισή ώρα *meesee ora*

half board (η) ημιδιατροφή *(ee) eemee-dhee-atrofee*

half-bottle η μικρή μπουκάλα *ee meekree boo-kala*

half fare το μισό εισιτήριο *to meeso eesee-teerio*

ham το ζαμπόν *to zambon*

hand το χέρι *to kheree*

handbag η τσάντα *ee tsanda*

handicapped οι ανάπηροι *ee anapeeree*

handkerchief το μαντήλι *to man-deelee*

hand luggage οι χειραποσκευές *ee kheera-poskeves*

hand-made χειροποίητος *kheero-pee-eetos*

happen συμβαίνω *seem-veno* || **what happened?** τι έγινε; *tee e-yeene?*

happy ευτυχισμένος *eftee-kheesmenos*

harbour το λιμάνι *to lee-manee*

hard σκληρός *skleeros*

hard-boiled *(egg)* σφιχτό *sfeekh-to*

hat το καπέλλο *to ka-pelo*

have *see* GRAMMAR

hay fever το αλλεργικό συνάχι *to aler-yeeko see-nakhee*

hazelnut το φουντούκι *to foon-dookee*

he αυτός *aftos*

head το κεφάλι *to ke-falee*

headache: I have a headache έχω πονοκέφαλο *ekho pono-kefalo*

hear ακούω *akoo-o*

heart η καρδιά *ee kardhee-a*

heart attack η καρδιακή προσβολή *ee kardhee-akee pros-volee*

heater η θερμάστρα *ee ther-mastra*

heating η θέρμανση *ee ther-mansee*

heavy βαρύς *varees*

hello γεια σας *ya sas*

help βοηθώ *vo-eetho* ‖ **help!** βοήθεια *vo-eethee-a*

herb το βότανο *to votano*

here εδώ *edho*

high ψηλός *pseelos*

high blood pressure η ψηλή πίεση *ee pseelee pee-esee*

high chair η ψηλή παιδική καρέκλα *ee pseelee pedhee-kee ka-rekla*

high tide η πλημμυρίδα *ee pleemee-reedha*

hill ο λόφος *o lofos* ‖ **(slope)** η πλαγιά *ee playee-a*

hill walking η ορειβασία *ee oree-vasee-a*

hire νοικιάζω *neekee-azo*

hit χτυπώ *khteepo*

hitchhike *n* το ωτοστόπ *to oto-stop*

hold κρατώ *krato*

hold-up η καθυστέρηση *ee kathee-stereesee*

hole η τρύπα *ee treepa*

holiday οι διακοπές *ee dhee-akopes* ‖ **I'm on holiday** είμαι διακοπές *ee-me dhee-akopes*

home το σπίτι *to speetee* ‖ **at home** στο σπίτι *sto speetee*

honey το μέλι *to melee*

honeymoon ο μήνας του μέλιτος *o meenas too melee-tos*

hope¹ *n* η ελπίδα *ee elpee-dha*

hope² *vb* ελπίζω *elpeezo*

hors d'oeuvre τα ορεκτικά *ta orek-teeka*

horse το άλογο *to alogho*

hose (in car) ο σωλήνας *o solee-nas*

hospital το νοσοκομείο *to noso-komee-o*

hot ζεστός *zestos* ‖ **I'm hot** ζεσταίνομαι *zeste-no-me* ‖ **it's hot** είναι ζεστό *ee-ne zesto*

hot water ζεστό νερό *zesto nero*

hotel το ξενοδοχείο *to kseno-dhokhee-o*

hour η ώρα *ee ora*

house το σπίτι *to speetee*

housewife η οικοκυρά *ee eeko-keera*

house wine κρασί χύμα *krasee kheema*

how πώς *pos* ‖ **how long?** πόσην ώρα; *poseen ora?* ‖ **how much?** πόσο; *poso?* ‖ **how many?** πόσα; *posa?* ‖ **how are you?** πώς είστε; *pos ee-ste?*

hungry: I'm hungry πεινώ *peeno*

hurry: I'm in a hurry βιάζομαι *vee-azome*

hurt: that hurts με πονάει *me pona-ee*

husband ο σύζυγος *o seezee-ghos*

hydrofoil το ιπτάμενο δελφίνι *to eepta-meno dhel-feenee*

I εγώ *egho*

ice ο πάγος *o paghos*

ice cream/ice lolly το παγωτό *to pagho-to*

iced *(drink)* παγωμένος *pagho-menos*

ice rink το παγοδρόμιο *to pagho-dhromee-o*

if αν *an*

ignition η ανάφλεξη *ee ana-fleksee*

ill άρρωστος *arostos*

immediately αμέσως *a-mesos*

important σπουδαίος *spoodhe-os*

impossible αδύνατο *adhee-nato*

in μέσα *mesa* II *(with countries, towns)* σε *se*

inch *see* CONVERSION CHARTS

included συμπεριλαμβανομένου *seemberee-lamvano-menoo*

indigestion η δυσπεψία *ee dheespepsee-a*

indoors μέσα *mesa*

infectious μεταδοτικός *meta-dhoteekhos*

information οι πληροφορίες *ee pleero-foree-es*

information office το γραφείο πληροφοριών *to ghrafee-o pleero-foree-on*

injection η ένεση *ee e-nesee*

injured τραυματισμένος *travma-teesmenos*

ink το μελάνι *to me-lanee*

insect το έντομο *to en-domo*

insect bite το τσίμπημα *to tseem-beema*

insect repellant η εντομοαπωθη-τική λοσιόν *ee endomo-apothee-teekee losee-on*

inside το εσωτερικό *to eso-tereeko* II inside the car μέσα στο αυτοκίνητο *mesa sto afto-keeneeto* II it's inside είναι μέσα *ee-ne mesa*

instant coffee στιγμιαίος καφές *steeghmee-eos ka-fes*

instead αντί *andee*

instructor ο εκπαιδευτής *o ekpe-dheftees*

insulin η ινσουλίνη *ee eensoo-leenee*

insurance η ασφάλεια *ee asfalee-a*

insurance certificate το πιστοποιητικό ασφάλειας *to peesto-pee-eeteeko asfalee-as*

interesting ενδιαφέρων *endhee-aferon*

international διεθνής *dhee-ethnees*

interpreter ο/η διερμηνέας *o/ee dhee-ermeene-as*

into σε *se*

invitation η πρόσκληση *ee pros-kleesee*

invite προσκαλώ *pros-kalo*

invoice το τιμολόγιο *to teemo*loyo*

Ireland η Ιρλανδία *ee eerlandhee-a*

Irish Ιρλανδός/Ιρλανδή *eerlan-dhos/eerlan-dhee*

iron *(metal)* το σίδερο *to see-dhero*

ironmonger's το σιδηροπωλείο *to seedheero-polee-o*

is *see* GRAMMAR

island το νησί *to neesee*

it *see* GRAMMAR

Italy η Ιταλία *ee eetalee-a*

itch η φαγούρα *ee fa-ghoora*

jack ο γρύλλος *o ghreelos*
jacket το σακκάκι *to sa-kakee*
jam η μαρμελάδα *ee marme-ladha*
jammed στριμωγμένος *streemogh-menos*
jar το βάζο *to vazo*
jazz η τζαζ *ee dzaz*
jeans το μπλου-τζην *to bloo-dzeen*
jelly το τζέλι *to dzelee*
jellyfish η μέδουσα *ee medhoo-sa*
jersey η φανέλα *ee fanela*
jeweller's το κοσμηματοπωλείο *to kosmee-mato-polee-o*
jewellery τα κοσμήματα *ta kosmee-mata*
job η δουλειά *ee dhoolee-a*
jogging: to go jogging πηγαίνω τζόκινγκ *pee-yeno dzoking*
join *(a club)* γίνομαι μέλος *gheenome melos*
joke το αστείο *to astee-o*
journey το ταξίδι *to takseedhee*
jug η κανάτα *ee kana-ta*
juice ο χυμός *o kheemos*
jump leads τα καλώδια μπαταρίας *ta kalodhee-a bataree-as*
junction *(crossroads)* η διασταύρωση *ee dhee-astav-rosee*
just: just two δύο *mono dhee-o* || I've just arrived μόλις έφτασα *molees eftasa*

keep κρατώ *krato*
kettle ο βραστήρας *o vrasteeras*
key το κλειδί *to kleedhee*
kidneys τα νεφρά *ta nefra*
kilo το κιλό *to keelo*
kilometre το χιλιόμετρο *to kheelee-ometro*
kind[1] *n (sort)* το είδος *to eedhos*
kind[2] *adj* καλός *kalos*
kiss φιλώ *feelo*
kitchen η κουζίνα *ee koo-zeena*
knife το μαχαίρι *to ma-kheree*
know ξέρω *ksero*

lace η νταντέλα *ee dan-dela*
ladder η σκάλα *ee skala*
Ladies' Γυναικών *yee-nekon*
lady η κυρία *ee keeree-a*
lager η μπύρα *ee beera*
lake η λίμνη *ee leemnee*
lamb το αρνάκι *to arnakee*
lamp η λάμπα *ee lamba*
lane το δρομάκι *to dhromakee*
language η γλώσσα *ee ghlosa*
large μεγάλος *me-ghalos*
last τελευταίος *telef-teos*
last week η περασμένη βδομάδα *ee perasmena vdhomadha*
late *(in the day)* αργά *argha* || I am late *(for an appointment)* άργησα *argheesa* || the train is 10 minutes late το τραίνο έχει καθυστέρηση 10 λεπτών *to treno ekhee kathee-stereese dheka lepton*
later αργότερα *argho-tera*
laundry service η υπηρεσία πλυντηρίου *ee eepeeresee-a pleendeeree-oo*
lavatory το αποχωρητήριο *to apokhoree-teeree-o*
lawyer ο/η δικηγόρος *o/ee dheekee-ghoros*
laxative το καθαρτικό *to kathar-teeko*

lay-by η βοηθητική λωρίδα *ee vo-eetheeteekee loreedha*

lead *(electric)* το καλώδιο *to kalodhee-o*

leader *(guide)* ο/η ξεναγός *o/ee ksenaghos*

leak η διαρροή *ee dhee-aro-ee*

learn μαθαίνω *ma-theno*

least: at least τουλάχιστο *toola-kheesto*

leather το δέρμα *to dherma*

leave φεύγω *fev-gho*

left: (on/to the) left αριστερά *aree-stera*

left-luggage (office) φύλαξη αποσκευών *feelaxee apo-skevon*

leg το πόδι *to podhee*

lemon το λεμόνι *to lemonee*

lemonade η λεμονάδα *ee lemo-nadha*

lemon tea τσάι με λεμόνι *tsa-ee me lemonee*

lend δανείζω *dha-neezo*

lens ο φακός *o fakos*

less: less milk λιγότερο γάλα *leegho-tero ghala*

lesson το μάθημα *to mathee-ma*

let *(allow)* επιτρέπω *epee-trepo* || *(hire out)* ενοικιάζω *eneekee-azo*

letter το γράμμα *to ghrama*

lettuce το μαρούλι *to ma-roolee*

library η βιβλιοθήκη *ee veevlee-otheekee*

licence η άδεια *ee adhee-a*

lid το κάλυμα *to ka-leema*

lie down ξαπλώνω *ksa-plono*

lifeboat η ναυαγοσωστική λέμβος *ee navagho-sosteekee lemvos*

lifeguard ο ναυαγοσώστης *o navaghosostees*

life jacket το σωσίβιο *to soseevee-o*

lift το ασανσέρ *to asan-ser* || *(ski)* τελεφερίκ για σκιέρ *telefereek ya skee-er*

lift pass *(skiing)* το εισιτήριο *to eesee-teeree-o*

light το φως *to fos*

light bulb η λάμπα *ee lamba*

lighter *(to light a cigarette)* ο αναπτήρας *o anap-teeras*

like¹ *vb* **: I like** μου αρέσει *moo a-resee*

like²: like you σαν κι εσένα *san kesena*

lime *(fruit)* το λάιμ *to lime*

line η γραμμή *ee ghramee*

lip salve το προστατευτικό στικ *to prostatef-teeko stick*

lipstick το κραγιόν *to kra-yon*

liqueur το λικέρ *to leeker*

listen (to) ακούω *akoo-o*

litre το λίτρο *to leetro*

little μικρός *meekros* || **a little** λίγο *leegho*

live μένω *meno* || **he lives in London** μένει στο Λονδίνο *menee sto lon-dheeno*

liver το συκώτι *to see-kotee*

living room το σαλόνι *to salonee*

loaf το καρβέλι *to kar-velee*

lobster ο αστακός *o asta-kos*

local τοπικός *topee-kos*

lock¹ *n* η κλειδαριά *ee kleedharee-a*

lock² *vb* κλειδώνω *kleedhono* || **I'm locked out** κλειδώθηκα έξω kleedho-theeka ekso

lollipop το γλειφιτζούρι to ghleefeed-**zoo**ree

London το Λονδίνο to lon-**dhee**no

long μακρύς ma**krees**

look at κοιτάζω kee-**ta**zo

look after φροντίζω fron-**dee**zo

look for γυρεύω yee-**rev**o

lorry το φορτηγό to fortee-**gho**

lose χάνω **kha**no

lost χαμένος kha-**me**nos ‖ **I have lost my wallet** έχασα το πορτοφόλι μου **e**khasa to porto**fo**li moo ‖ **I am lost** χάθηκα **kha**theeka

lost-property office το γραφείο απολεσθέντων αντικειμένων to ghra**fee**-o apoles-**then**don andeekee-**me**non

lot: a lot (of) πολύς po**lees**

lotion η λοσιόν ee losee-**on**

loud δυνατός dhee**na**-tos

lounge (at airport) η αίθουσα ee **ethoo**-sa ‖ (in hotel, house) το σαλόνι to sa**lo**nee

love αγαπώ agha-**po**

lovely ωραίος o**re**-os

low χαμηλός khamee-**los**

low-alcohol beer μπύρα χαμηλή σε οινόπνευμα **bee**ra khamee**lee** se een**op**nevma

low tide η άμπωτη ee **am**-botee

luggage οι αποσκευές ee apo-**skeves**

luggage allowance το επιτρεπόμενο βάρος αποσκευών to epeetre-**po**meno **va**ros apo-**skev**on

luggage rack ο χώρος αποσκευών o **kho**ros apo-**skev**on

luggage tag η ετικέτα ee etee**ke**ta

luggage trolley το καρότσι αποσκευών to ka-**rot**see apo-**skev**on

lunch το μεσημεριανό to mesee-meree-**a**no

luxury η πολυτέλεια ee polee-te**lee**-a

macaroni τα μακαρόνια ta makaronee-**a**

madam η κυρία ee kee**ree**-a

magazine το περιοδικό to peree-o**dhee**ko

maid η καμαριέρα ee kamaree-**e**ra

main κύριος **kee**ree-os

mains (electric) ο κεντρικός αγωγός o kendree-**kos** agho-**ghos**

make κάνω **ka**no

make-up το μακιγιάζ to makee-**yaz**

mallet το ξύλινο σφυρί to **ksee**leeno sfee**ree**

man (mankind) ο άνθρωπος o **an**-thropos ‖ (as opposed to woman) ο άνδρας o **an**dhras

manager ο διευθυντής o dhee-ef-thee**ndees**

many πολλοί po**lee** ‖ **many people** πολλοί άνθρωποι po**lee** an-**thro**pee

map ο χάρτης o **khar**tees

margarine η μαργαρίνη ee margha-**ree**nee

market η αγορά ee agho-**ra**

market day η μέρα της αγοράς ee **me**ra tees agho-**ras**

marmalade η μαρμελάδα ee marme-**la**dha

married παντρεμένος pandre-**me**nos

Martini το μαρτίνι to mar**tee**nee

marzipan το γκλασάρισμα

αμυγδάλου *to glasa-reesma ameegh-dhaloo*

mascara μάσκαρα *maskara*

mass *(religious service)* η Θεία Λειτουργία *ee thee-a leetoor-yee-a*

matches τα σπίρτα *ta speerta*

material το υλικό *to eelee-ko*

matter: it doesn't matter δεν πειράζει *dhen pee-razee* || **what's the matter with you?** τι έχεις; *tee ehees?*

mayonnaise η μαγιονέζα *ee mayo-neza*

meal το γεύμα *to yevma*

mean εννοώ *eno-o*

measles η ιλαρά *ee eelara*

meat το κρέας *to kre-as*

mechanic ο μηχανικός *o meekha-neekos*

medicine το γιατρικό *to yatree-ko*

Mediterranean η Μεσόγειος *ee meso-yee-os*

medium *(wine)* μέτριο γλυκύ *metree-o ghleekee* || *(steak)* μέτριο *metree-o* || *(size)* μέτριο *metree-o*

meet συναντώ *seenan-do*

melon το πεπόνι *to pe-ponee* || *(watermelon)* το καρπούζι *to kar-poozee*

melt λυώνω *lee-ono*

member το μέλος *to melos*

men οι άντρες *ee antres*

menu το μενού *to menoo*

meringue η μαρέγκα *ee marenka*

message το μήνυμα *to mee-neema*

metal το μέταλο *to metalo*

meter ο μετρητής *o metree-tees*

metre το μέτρο *to metro*

migraine η ημικρανία *ee eemee-kranee-a*

mile *see* **CONVERSION CHARTS**

milk το γάλα *to ghala*

milk shake το μιλκσέικ *to meelk-se-eek*

millimetre το χιλιοστόμετρο *to kheelee-ostometro*

million το εκατομμύριο *to ekato-meeree-o*

mince ο κιμάς *o keemas*

mind: do you mind if …? σας ενοχλεί αν …; *sas enokh-lee an …?*

mineral water το επιτραπέζιο νερό *to epee-trapezee-o nero* || *(sparkling)* το μεταλλικό νερό *to meta-leeko nero*

minimum ελάχιστος *ela-kheestos*

minister *(church)* ο ιερέας *o ee-ere-as*

minor road ο δευτερεύων δρόμος *o dhefte-revon dhromos*

mint *(herb)* ο δυόσμος *o dhee-osmos*

minute το λεπτό *to lepto*

mirror ο καθρέφτης *o kath-reftees*

miss *(train, etc)* χάνω *khano*

Miss η Δεσποινίς *ee dhespee-nees*

missing χαμένος *kha-menos*

mistake το λάθος *to lathos*

misunderstanding η παρεξήγηση *ee parekseegheesee*

modern μοντέρνος *mondernos*

moisturizer το μοίστιαράιζερ *to moystoo-ryzer*

monastery το μοναστήρι *to mona-steeree*

money τα χρήματα *ta khree-mata*

109

money order η ταχυδρομική επιταγή *ee takhee-dhromeekee epee-tayee*

month ο μήνας *o meenas*

monument το μνημείο *to mneemee-o*

mop η σφουγγαρίστρα *ee sfoonga-reestra*

more περισσότερος *peree-soteros* || **more bread** κι' άλλο ψωμί *kee-alo psomee*

morning το πρωί *to pro-ee*

mosque το τζαμί *to dzamee*

mosquito το κουνούπι *to koo-noopee*

most ο περισσότερος *o peree-soteros*

mother η μητέρα *ee mee-tera*

motor η μηχανή *ee mee-khanee*

motorbike η μοτοσυκλέτα *ee moto-seekleta*

motorboat η βενζινάκατος *ee venzee-natakos*

motorway ο αυτοκινητόδρομος *o afto-keenee-todhromos*

mountain το βουνό *to voono*

mousse το μους *to moos*

mouth το στόμα *to stoma*

move κινούμαι *keenoo-me*

Mr Κύριος *keeree-os*

Mrs Κυρία *keeree-a*

much πολύς *polees* || **too much** πολύ *polee* || **very much** πάρα πολύ *para polee*

mumps οι μαγουλάδες *ee maghooladhes*

museum το μουσείο *to moosee-o*

mushroom το μανιτάρι *to manee-taree*

music η μουσική *ee mooseekee*

mussel το μύδι *to meedhee*

must: I must go πρέπει να πάω *prepee na pa-o* || **you must go** πρέπει να πας *prepee na pas* || **he/she must go** πρέπει να πάει *prepee na pa-ee*

mustard η μουστάρδα *ee moo-stardha*

mutton το αρνί *to arnee*

nail (metal) το καρφί *to karfee* || (on finger, toe) το νύχι *to neekhee*

nail polish το βερνίκι *to verneekee*

nail polish remover το ασετόν *to aseton*

nailbrush η βούρτσα των νυχιών *ee voortsa ton neekhee-on*

naked γυμνός *yeemnos*

name το όνομα *to onoma*

napkin η πετσέτα *ee pet-seta*

nappy η πάνα *ee pana*

narrow στενός *stenos*

nationality η εθνικότητα *ee ethnee-koteeta*

navy blue μπλε *ble*

near κοντά *konda*

necessary απαραίτητος *apare-teetos*

neck ο λαιμός *o lemos*

necklace το κολιέ *to kolee-e*

need: I need … χρειάζομαι … *khree-azo-me …*

needle το βελόνι *to ve-lonee* || **a needle and thread** βελόνι και κλωστή *velonee ke klostee*

negative (photography) αρνητικός *arnee-teekos*

neighbour ο γείτονας/η γειτόνισσα *o yee-tonas/ee yeeto-neesa*

never ποτέ *po-te* || **I never go there** δεν πηγαίνω ποτέ εκεί *dhen peegheno pote ekee*

new καινούργιος *kenoor-yos*

news *(TV, radio)* οι ειδήσεις *ee eedhee-sees*

newsagent's το πρακτορείο εφημερίδων *to prakto-reeo efee-mereedhon*

newspaper η εφημερίδα *ee efee-mereedha*

New Year ο καινούργιος χρόνος *o kenoor-yos khronos* || **happy New Year!** ευτυχισμένος ο καινούργιος χρόνος! *eftee-khees-menos o kenoor-yos khronos*

New Zealand η Νέα Ζηλανδία *ee ne-a zeelandhee-a*

next επόμενος *epomenos*

nice ωραίος *ore-os*

night η νύχτα *ee neekh-ta*

nightclub το νυχτερινό κέντρο *to neekh-tereeno kendro*

nightdress το νυχτικό *to neekh-teeko*

no όχι *okhee*

nobody κανένας *ka-nenas*

noisy θορυβώδης *thoree-vodhees*

non-alcoholic μη οινοπνευματώδης *mee eenop-nevma-todhees*

none κανένα *ka-nena*

non-smoking μη καπνίζοντες *mee kapnee-zondes*

north ο βορράς *o voras*

Nothern Ireland η Βόρεια

Ιρλανδία *ee voree-a eerlandhee-a*

not μη *mee* || **I am not** δεν είμαι *dhen ee-me*

note *(bank note)* το χαρτονόμισμα *to khartonomeesma* || *(letter)* το σημείωμα *to seemee-oma*

note pad το σημειωματάριο *to seemee-omataree-o*

nothing τίποτα *tee-pota*

now τώρα *tora*

number ο αριθμός *o areeth-mos*

nurse η νοσοκόμα *ee noso-koma*

nursery slopes *(skiing)* η πλαγιά για αρχάριους *ee pla-ya ya arkharee-oos*

nut *(peanut)* το φυστίκι *to feesteekee* || *(walnut)* το καρύδι *to kareedhee* || *(hazelnut)* το φουντούκι *to foontookee* || *(for bolt)* το παξιμάδι *to paksee-madhee*

occasionally κάπου-κάπου *kapoo-kapoo*

of: of course βέβαια *ve-ve-a*

off *(light, machine, etc)* σβυστός *sveestos* || **it's off** *(rotten)* είναι χαλασμένο *ee-ne khalas-meno* || **to get off the bus** κατεβαίνω από το λεωφορείο *ka-te-veno apo to leoforee-o*

offer προσφέρω *pros-fero*

office το γραφείο *to ghrafee-o*

often συχνά *seekh-na*

oil το λάδι *to ladhee*

oil filter το φίλτρο του λαδιού *to feeltro too ladhee-oo*

ointment η αλοιφή *ee aleefee*

OK εντάξει *en-daksee*

old *(person)* ηλικιωμένος *eeleekee-*

omenos || (thing) παλιός palee-os || **how old are you?** πόσων χρόνων είστε; poson khronon ee-ste?

olive oil το ελαιόλαδο to ele-oladho

olives οι ελιές ee elee-es

omelette η ομελέτα ee omeleta

on (light, machine, etc) ανοικτός aneek-tos || **on (the table)** στο (τραπέζι) sto (tra-pezee)

once μια φορά mee-a fora

one ένας/μία/ένα enas/mee-a/ena

one-way (street) ο μονόδρομος o mono-dhromos || (ticket) το απλό εισιτήριο to aplo eesee-teeree-o

onion το κρεμμύδι to kre-meedhee

only μόνο mono

open[1] vb ανοίγω anee-gho

open[2] adj ανοικτός aneek-tos

opera η όπερα ee o-pera

operator (telephone) η τηλεφωνήτρια ee teelefo-neetree-a

opposite απέναντι ape-nandee

or ή ee

orange (fruit) το πορτοκάλι to porto-kalee || (colour) πορτοκαλί porto-kalee

orange juice ο χυμός πορτοκαλιού o kheemos porto-kalee-oo

order παραγγέλω paran-gelo

original αρχικός arkhee-kos

Orthodox (religion) ορθόδοξος ortho-dhoksos

other άλλος alos

ounce see CONVERSION CHARTS

out (light, etc) σβησμένος svees-menos || **he's out** λείπει leepee

outdoors στην ύπαιθρο steen ee-pethro

outside έξω ekso

oven ο φούρνος o foornos

over πάνω από pano apo || **over there** εκεί πέρα ekee pera

overcharge παίρνω παραπάνω perno para-pano

owe: you owe me μου χρωστάς moo khrostas

owner ο ιδιοκτήτης o eedhee-okteetees

oyster το στρείδι to streedhee

pack πακετάρω paketaro

package το δέμα to dhema

package tour η οργανωμένη εκδρομή ee orghanomenee ek-dhromee

packet το πακέτο to pa-keto

paddling pool η λιμνούλα για παιδιά ee leem-noola ya pedhee-a

paid πληρωμένος pleero-menos

painful οδυνηρός odhee-neeros

painkiller το παυσίπονο to pafsee-pono

painting ο πίνακας o peenakas

pair το ζευγάρι to zev-gharee

palace το παλάτι to palatee

pan η κατσαρόλα ee katsa-rola

pancake η τηγανίτα ee teegha-neeta

panties η κυλότα ee keelota

pants το σώβρακο to sovra-ko

paper το χαρτί to khartee

paraffin η παραφίνη ee para-feenee

parcel το δέμα to dhema

pardon παρακαλώ para-kalo || **I beg your pardon** με συγχωρείτε me seenkho-reete parent ο γονιός *o ghonee-os*

park[1] *n* το πάρκο *to parko*

park[2] *vb (in car)* παρκάρω *parkaro*

parsley ο μαϊντανός *o ma-eendanos*

part το μέρος *to meros*

party *(group)* η ομάδα *ee omadha* || *(celebration)* το πάρτυ *to party*

passenger ο επιβάτης *o epee-vatees*

passport το διαβατήριο *to dhee-avateeree-o*

passport control ο έλεγχος διαβατηρίων *o elen-khos dhee-avateeree-on*

pasta τα μακαρόνια *ta makaronee-a*

pastry η ζύμη *ee zeemee* || *(cake)* το γλύκισμα *to ghlee-keesma*

pâté το πατέ *to pate*

path το μονοπάτι *to mono-patee*

pay πληρώνω *plee-rono*

payment η πληρωμή *ee plee-romee*

peach το ροδάκινο *to rodha-keeno*

peanut το φυστίκι *to fee-steekee*

pear το αχλάδι *to akh-ladhee*

peas τα μπιζέλια *ta beezelee-a*

peel ξεφλουδίζω *ksefloo-dheezo*

peg *(for tent)* ο πάσσαλος σκηνής *o pasalos skeenees* || *(for clothes)* το μανταλάκι *to manda-lakee*

pen η πένα *ee pena*

pencil το μολύβι *to mo-leevee*

penicillin η πενικιλλίνη *ee penee-keeleenee*

penknife ο σουγιάς *o soo-yas*

pensioner ο/η συνταξιούχος *o/ee seendaksee-ookhos*

pepper *(vegetable or spice)* το

πιπέρι *to pee-peree*

per: per hour την ώρα *teen ora*

perfect τέλειος *telee-os*

performance η παράσταση *ee para-stasee*

perfume το άρωμα *to aroma*

perhaps ίσως *eesos*

period *(menstruation)* η περίοδος *ee peree-odhos*

perm η περμανάντ *ee permanand*

permit άδεια *adhee-a*

person το πρόσωπο *to pro-sopo*

petrol η βενζίνη *ee ven-zeenee*

petrol station το πρατήριο βενζίνης *to prateeree-o ven-zeenees*

phone *see* telephone

photocopy η φωτοτυπία *ee fototee-pee-a*

photograph η φωτογραφία *ee foto-ghrafee-a*

picnic το πικ-νικ *to picnic*

picture η εικόνα *ee eekona*

pie η πίτα *ee peeta*

piece το κομμάτι *to ko-matee*

pill το χάπι *to khapee*

pillow το μαξιλάρι *to maksee-laree*

pillowcase η μαξιλαροθήκη *ee maksee-laro-theekee*

pin η καρφίτσα *ee karfeet-sa*

pine το πεύκο *to pefko*

pineapple ο ανανάς *o ananas*

pink ροζ *roz*

pint *see* CONVERSION CHARTS

pipe η πίπα *ee peepa*

pistachio nut το φυστίκι Αιγίνης *to fee-steekee e-yeenees*

plane το αεροπλάνο *to aero-plano*

plaster *(for cut)* ο λευκοπλάστης *o lefko-plastees* || *(for broken limb)* ο γύψος *o yeepsos*

plastic πλαστικός *plastee-kos*

plate το πιάτο *to pee-ato*

platform η αποβάθρα *ee apo-vathra*

play παίζω *pezo*

playroom το δωμάτιο των παιδιών *to dhomatee-o ton pedhee-on*

please παρακαλώ *para-kalo*

pleased ευχαριστημένος *efhareesteemenos*

pliers η πένσα *ee pensa*

plug *(electric)* η πρίζα *ee preeza*

plum το δαμάσκηνο *to dhama-skeeno*

plumber ο υδραυλικός *o eedrav-leekos*

points *(in car)* οι πλατίνες *ee pla-teenes*

police η αστυνομία *ee astee-nomee-a*

policeman ο αστυνομικός *o astee-nomeekos*

police station το αστυνομικό τμήμα *to astee-nomeeko tmeema*

polish *(for shoes)* το βερνίκι *to ver-neekee*

polluted μολυσμένος *molees-menos*

pony trekking η ιππασία *ee eepasee-a*

pool *(for swimming)* η πισίνα *ee pee-seena*

popular δημοφιλής *dheemo-feelees* || *(fashionable)* κοσμικός *kosmee-kos*

pork το χοιρινό *to kheeree-no*

port *(harbour)* το λιμάνι *to lee-manee*

porter ο αχθοφόρος *o akh-thoforos*

possible δυνατός *dheena-tos*

post *(letter)* ταχυδρομώ *takhee-dhromo*

postbox το ταχυδρομικό κουτί *to takhee-dhromeeko kootee*

postcard η καρτ ποστάλ *ee kart-postal*

postcode ο κωδικός *o kodheekos*

post office το ταχυδρομείο *to takhee-dhromee-o*

pot η κατσαρόλα *ee katsa-rola*

potato η πατάτα *ee patata*

pottery η κεραμική *ee kera-meekee*

pound *(money)* η λίρα *ee leera* || *(weight)* see **CONVERSION CHARTS**

powdered milk το γάλα σε σκόνη *to ghala se skonee*

pram το καροτσάκι *to karot-sakee*

prawn η γαρίδα *ee gha-reedha*

prefer προτιμώ *pro-teemo*

pregnant έγγυος *engee-os*

prepare ετοιμάζω *etee-mazo*

prescription η συνταγή *ee seenda-yee*

present *(gift)* το δώρο *to dhoro*

pretty ωραίος *ore-os*

price η τιμή *ee teemee*

price list ο τιμοκατάλογος *o teemokataloghos*

priest ο παπάς *o papas*

private ιδιωτικός *eedhee-oteekos*

probably πιθανώς *peetha-nos*

problem το πρόβλημα *to prov-leema*

programme το πρόγραμμα *to pro-ghrama*

pronounce προφέρω *pro-fero* ǁ
how do you pronounce this? πώς
το προφέρετε; *pos to profere-te?*

Protestant διαμαρτυρόμενος *dhee-amartee-romenos*

prune το δαμάσκηνο *to dhama-skeeno*

public δημόσιος *dheemosee-os*

public holiday η γιορτή *ee yortee*

pudding η πουτίγκα *ee poo-teenga*

pull τραβώ *travo*

pullover το πουλόβερ *to poolover*

puncture το τρύπημα *to tree-peema*

purple πορφυρός *porfee-ros*

purse το τσαντάκι *to tsan-dakee*

push σπρώχνω *sprokh-no*

put βάζω *vazo* ǁ **to put down** βάζω
κάτω *vazo kato*

pyjamas οι πιζάμες *ee pee-za-mes*

queue η ουρά *ee oora*

quick γρήγορος *ghreeghoros*

quickly γρήγορα *ghree-ghora*

quiet ήσυχος *eesee-khos*

quilt *(duvet)* το πάπλωμα *to paplo-ma*

quite *(rather)* μάλλον *malon* ǁ
(completely) απολύτως *apo-leetos*

rabbit το κουνέλι *to koo-nelee*

racket η ρακέτα *ee raketa*

radiator το καλοριφέρ *to kalo-reefer*

radio το ραδιόφωνο *to radhee-ofono*

radish το ραπανάκι *to rapa-nakee*

railway station ο σιδηροδρομικός
σταθμός *o seedheero-dhromeekos
stath-mos*

rain η βροχή *ee vrokhee*

raincoat το αδιάβροχο *to adhee-avrokho*

raining: it's raining βρέχει *vrekhee*

raisin η σταφίδα *ee sta-feedha*

rare σπάνιος *spanee-os* ǁ *(steak)*
μισοψημένος *meesop-seemenos*

raspberries τα βατόμουρα *ta vato-moora*

rate ο ρυθμός *o reeth-mos* ǁ **rate of
exchange** η τιμή του
συναλλάγματος *ee teemee too
seenalagh-matos*

raw ωμός *omos*

razor το ξυράφι *to ksee-rafee*

razor blades οι λεπίδες *ee le-peedhes*

ready έτοιμος *etee-mos*

real πραγματικός *praghma-teekos*

receipt η απόδειξη *ee apo-dheeksee*

recently τελευταία *telefte-a*

reception (desk) η ρεσεψιόν *ee
resepsee-on*

recipe η συνταγή *ee seenda-yee*

recommend συνιστώ *seenee-sto*

record *(music, etc)* ο δίσκος *o
dheeskos*

red κόκκινος *kokee-nos*

reduction η έκπτωση *ee ek-ptosee*

refill το ανταλλακτικό *to anda-lakteeko*

refund η επιστροφή χρημάτων *ee
epee-strofee khree-maton*

registered *(letter)* συστημένο seesteemeno

regulations οι κανονισμοί ee kanoneesmee

reimburse αποζημιώνω apozeemee-ono

relations *(family)* οι συγγενείς ee seenkenees

relax ξεκουράζομαι ksekoo-razo-me

reliable *(person)* αξιόπιστος akseeopeestos || *(car, method)* δοκιμασμένος dhokee-masmenos

remain απομένω apo-meno

remember θυμάμαι theemame

rent ενοικιάζω eneekee-azo

rental το νοίκι to neekee

repair επιδιορθώνω epeedhee-orthono

repeat επαναλαμβάνω epanalamvano

reservation το κλείσιμο to kleeseemo

reserve προκρατώ pro-krato

reserved κρατημένος kratee-menos

rest[1] *n* ξεκούραση ksekoo-rasee || **the rest** οι υπόλοιποι ee eepoleepee

rest[2] *vb* ξεκουράζομαι ksekoo-razo-me

restaurant το εστιατόριο to esteeatoree-o

restaurant car το βαγκόν-ρεστωράν to vagon-restoran

return *(go back, give back)* επιστρέφω epee-strefo

return ticket το εισιτήριο με επιστροφή to eesee-teeree-o me epee-strofee

reverse-charge call κλήση πληρωτέα από τον παραλήπτη kleesee pleerotea apo ton paraleeptee

rheumatism οι ρευματισμοί ee rhevma-teesmee

rice το ρύζι to reezee

riding *(equestrian)* η ιππασία ee eepasee-a

right *(correct, accurate)* σωστός sostos || **(on/to the) right** δεξιά dheksee-a

ring το δαχτυλίδι to dhakhtee-leedhee

ripe ώριμος oree-mos

river το ποτάμι to po-tamee

road ο δρόμος o dhromos

road map ο οδικός χάρτης o odhee-kos khartees

roast το ψητό to pseeto

roll *(of bread)* το ψωμάκι to psomakee

roof η στέγη ee ste-yee

roof rack η σχάρα ee skhara

room *(in house, etc)* το δωμάτιο to dhomatee-o || *(space)* ο χώρος o khoros

room service η υπηρεσία δωματίου ee eepee-resee-a dhomatee-oo

rope το σχοινί to skheenee

rosé ροζέ rose

rough *(sea)* τρικυμισμένη treekee-meesmenee

round *(shape)* στρογγυλός strongeelos || **round the house/Greece** γύρω στο σπίτι/στην Ελλάδα yeero sto speetee/steen eladha || **round the corner** στη γωνία stee ghonee-a

route ο δρόμος *o dhromos*
rowing boat βάρκα με κουπιά *varka me koopee-a*
rubber το λάστιχο *to lastee-ko* ‖ **rubber band** το λαστιχάκι *to lastee-khakee*
rubbish τα σκουπίδια *ta skoopeedhee-a*
rucksack ο σάκκος *o sakos*
ruins τα ερείπια *ta ereepee-a*
rum το ρούμι *to roomee*
run *(skiing)* η διαδρομή του σκι *ee dhee-adhromee too skee*
rush hour η ώρα συνοστισμού *ee ora seeno-steesmoo*

safe[1] *adj (medicine)* αβλαβής *avlavees* ‖ *(beach)* ακίνδυνος *akeendheenos*
safe[2] *n* το χρηματοκιβώτιο *to khreemato-keevotee-o*
safety pin η παραμάνα *ee paramana*
sailboard σέιλμπορτ *to sailboard*
sailing η ιστιοπλοΐα *ee eestee-oplo-ee-a*
salad η σαλάτα *ee salata*
salad dressing το λαδολέμονο *to ladho-lemono*
salmon ο σολομός *o solo-mos*
salt το αλάτι *to alatee*
same ίδιος *eedhee-os*
sand η άμμος *ee amos*
sandals τα πέδιλα *ta pedhee-la*
sandwich το σάντουϊτς *to sandoo-eets*
sanitary towel η σερβιέτα *ee servee-eta*

sardine η σαρδέλα *ee sardhela*
sauce η σάλτσα *ee saltsa*
saucepan η κατσαρόλα *ee katsarola*
saucer το πιατάκι *to pee-atakee*
sauna το σάουνα *to sa-oona*
sausage το λουκάνικο *to lookaneeko*
savoury πικάντικος *peekan-deekos*
say λέω *le-o*
scallop το χτένι *to khtenee*
scampi μεγάλες γαρίδες *meghales ghareedhes*
scarf *(long)* το κασκόλ *to kaskol* ‖ *(square)* το σάλι *to salee*
school το σχολείο *to skholee-o* ‖ *(for 12-15 year-olds)* το γυμνάσιο *to yeemnasee-o* ‖ *(for 15-18 year-olds)* το λύκειο *to leekee-o*
scissors το ψαλίδι *to psa-leedhee*
Scotland η Σκωτία *ee skotee-a*
Scottish Σκωτσέζος/Σκωτσέζα *skotsezos/skot-seza*
screw η βίδα *ee veeda*
screwdriver το κατσαβίδι *to katsaveedhee*
sculpture το γλυπτό *to ghleep-to*
sea η θάλασσα *ee tha-lasa*
seafood τα θαλασσινά *ta thalaseena*
seasickness η ναυτία *ee naftee-a*
seaside η θάλασσα *ee tha-lasa*
season ticket το διαρκές εισιτήριο *to dhee-arkhes eesee-teeree-o*
seat *(in theatre)* η θέση *ee thesee* ‖ *(in car, etc)* το κάθισμα *to katheesma*

second δεύτερος **dhef**-teros ||
second class (ticket, etc) δεύτερη
θέση **dhef**teree **thesee**

see βλέπω **vlepo**

self-service αυτοψωνίζετε afto-
psonee-zete

sell πουλώ **poolo**

Sellotape ® το σελοτέιπ to selote-
eep

send στέλνω **stelno**

senior citizen ο/η συνταξιούχος
o/ee seentaksee-**ookhos**

separate χωριστός khoree-**stos**

serious σοβαρός sova-ros

serve σερβίρω ser-**veero**

service (in restaurant, etc) η
υπηρεσία ee eepee-re**see**-a

service charge το ποσοστό
υπηρεσίας to poso-**sto** eepee-re**see**-
as

set menu το καθορισμένο μενού to
kathorees**meno menoo**

shade η σκιά ee skee-**a**

shallow ρηχός **reekhos**

shampoo το σαμπουάν to samboo-
an

shampoo and set λούσιμο και
οντουλάρισμα **looseemo** ke
ontoola**reesma**

shandy το σάντυ to **santee**

share μοιράζω mee-**razo**

shave ξυρίζομαι ksee**ree**-zo-me

shaving cream η κρέμα
ξυρίσματος ee **krema** ksee**rees**-
matos

she αυτή af**tee**

sheet το σεντόνι to sen-**donee**

shellfish τα θαλασσινά ta thala-
seena

ship το πλοίο to **plee**-o

shirt το πουκάμισο to pooka-**meeso**

shock absorber το αμορτισέρ to
amor-**teeser**

shoe το παπούτσι to pa-**pootsee**

shop το μαγαζί to magha-**zee**

shopping τα ψώνια ta **psonee**-a ||
to go shopping ψωνίζω pso-**neezo**

short κοντός **kondos**

short cut ο συντομότερος δρόμος
o seendo-**moteros dhromos**

shorts τα σορτς ta shorts

show[1] n (in theatre, etc) η
παράσταση ee para-stasee

show[2] vb δείχνω **dheekh**-no

shower (in bath) το ντους to doos ||
(rain) η μπόρα ee **bora**

shrimp η γαρίδα ee gha-**reedha**

sick (ill) άρρωστος **aro**-stos || **to be
sick** (vomit) κάνω εμετό **kano** eme-
to

sightseeing: to go sightseeing
επισκέπτομαι τα αξιοθέατα epee-
skepto-me ta aksee-o**the**-ata

sign (roadsign, notice, etc) η
πινακίδα ee peena**keedha**

signature η υπογραφή ee eepo-
ghra**fee**

silk το μετάξι to me-**taksee**

silver ασημένιος asee-**menee**-os

similar παρόμοιος paro**mee**-os

simple απλός a**plos**

single (not married) ελεύθερος elef-
theros || (not double) μονός **monos**

single bed το μονό κρεβάτι to
mono kre**vatee**

single room το μονόκλινο
δωμάτιο to mono-**kleeno**
dho**matee**-o

sink ο νεροχύτης ο nero-**khee**tees

sir κύριε **kee**ree-e

sister η αδελφή ee adhel-**fee**

sit (down) κάθομαι **katho**-me

size (of clothes, shoes) το μέγεθος to me-yethos

skate (sportswear) το πατίνι to pa-**tee**nee

skating το πατινάζ to pateenaz

ski[1] n το σκι to skee

ski[2] vb κάνω σκι **kano** skee

ski jacket το σακκάκι του σκι to sakhakee too skee

ski pants το παντελόνι του σκι to pande-**lo**nee too skee

ski pole το ραβδί του σκι to rav-**dhee** too skee

ski run η διαδρομή του σκι ee dhee-adhro**mee** too skee

ski suit τα ρούχα του σκι ta **roo**kha too skee

skimmed milk το αποβουτυρωμένο γάλα to apo-vootee-romeno **gha**la

skin το δέρμα to **dher**ma

skin diving το υποβρύχιο κολύμπι to eepovreekhee-o ko**lee**mpee

skirt η φούστα ee **foo**sta

sleep κοιμούμαι keemoo-me

sleeper το βαγκόν-λι to **vagon**-lee

sleeping bag το σλίπιγκ-μπαγκ to sleeping bag

sleeping pill το υπνωτικό χάπι to eepno-tee**ko kha**pee

slice η φέτα ee **fe**ta

slide (photography) το σλάιντ to slide

slipper η παντόφλα ee pan-**do**fla

slippery γλιστερός ghlee-ste**ros**

slow σιγά **see**gha

small μικρός **mee**kros

smaller (than) μικρότερος (από) **mee**kro-teros (apo)

smell η μυρωδιά ee meerodhee-**a**

smoke[1] n ο καπνός o kap**nos**

smoke[2] vb καπνίζω kap-**nee**zo

smoked καπνιστός kap-nee**stos**

snack bar το σνακ-μπαρ to snack-bar

snorkel ο αναπνευστικός σωλήνας o anap-nevstee-**kos** so-**lee**nas

snow το χιόνι to khee-**o**nee

snowed up αποκλεισμένος από το χιόνι apo-klees**me**nos apo to khee-**o**nee

snowing: it's snowing χιονίζει khee-o**nee**zee

so γι' αυτό ya**fto** || so much τόσο πολύ **to**so po**lee** || so pretty τόσο ωραίος **to**so o-**re**-os

soap το σαπούνι to sa-**poo**nee

soap powder η σαπουνόσκονη ee sapoo-**no**skonee

sober ξεμέθυστος ksemethee-stos

sock η κάλτσα ee **kal**tsa

socket (electrical) η πρίζα ee **pree**za

soda (water) η σόδα ee **so**dha

soft μαλακός mala-**kos**

soft drink το αναψυκτικό to anapseek-**tee**ko

some μερικοί meree-**kee**

someone κάποιος **ka**pee-os

something κάτι **ka**tee

sometimes κάποτε **ka**po-te

son ο γιος o yos

song το τραγούδι to tra-**ghoo**dhee

soon σύντομα **seen**-doma || as soon

as possible το συντομότερο *to seendo-mo-tero* || **sooner** νωρίτερα *noree-tera*

sore: it's sore πονάει *pona-ee*

sorry: I'm sorry *(apology)* συγγνώμη *seegh-nomee* || *(regret)* λυπούμαι *leepoo-me*

sort το είδος *to eedhos*

soup η σούπα *ee soopa*

south ο νότος *o notos*

souvenir το σουβενίρ *to sooveneer*

space το διάστημα *to dhee-asteema* || *(room)* ο χώρος *o khoros*

spade το φτυάρι *to ftee-aree*

spanner το κλειδί *to kleedhee*

spare wheel η ρεζέρβα *ee rezerva*

spark plug το μπουζί *to boozee*

sparkling *(wine)* αφρώδης *afrodhees*

speak μιλώ *meelo*

special ειδικός *eedhee-kos*

speciality *(in restaurant)* σπεσιαλιτέ *spesee-alee-te*

speed η ταχύτητα *ee takhee-teeta*

speed limit το όριο ταχύτητας *to oree-o takhee-teetas*

spell γράφω *ghrafo* || **how do you spell it?** πώς γράφεται; *pos ghra-fe-te?*

spicy αρωματισμένος *aroma-teesmenos*

spinach το σπανάκι *to spa-nakee*

spirits τα οινοπνευματώδη ποτά *ta eenop-nevma-todhee pota*

sponge το σφουγγάρι *to sfoon-garee*

spoon το κουτάλι *to koo-talee*

sport το σπορ *to spor*

spring *(season)* η άνοιξη *ee aneek-see*

square *(in town)* η πλατεία *ee platee-a*

squash *(sport)* το σκουός *to skoo-os* || **orange squash** η πορτοκαλάδα *ee porto-kaladha* || **lemon squash** η λεμονάδα *ee lemo-nadha*

stairs η σκάλα *ee skala*

stalls *(in theatre)* η πλατεία *ee platee-a*

stamp το γραμματόσημο *to ghrama-toseemo*

start αρχίζω *ar-kheezo*

starter *(in meal)* το ορεκτικό *to orek-teeko*

station ο σταθμός *o stath-mos*

stationer's το χαρτοπωλείο *to kharto-polee-o*

stay μένω *meno*

steak το μπιφτέκι *to beeftekee*

steep ανηφορικός *anee-foreekos*

sterling η αγγλική λίρα *ee anglee-kee leera*

stew (το) κρέας με χορταρικά στην κατσαρόλα *(to) kreas me khorta-reeka steen katsa-rola*

steward *(on a ship)* ο καμαρότος *o kama-rotos* || *(on plane)* ο αεροσυνοδός *o aero-seenodhos*

stewardess *(on plane)* η αεροσυνοδός *ee aero-seenodhos*

sticking plaster ο λευκοπλάστης *o lefko-plastees*

still *(yet)* ακόμα *akoma* || *(immobile)* ακίνητος *akee-neetos*

sting το κέντρισμα *to ken-dreesma*

stockings οι κάλτσες *ee kalt-ses*

stomach το στομάχι *to sto-makhee*

stomach upset η στομαχική διαταραχή *ee stoma-kheekee dhee-ata-rakhee* stop σταματώ stama-**to**

stopover *(in air travel)* ο σταθμός *o* stath-**mos**

storm η καταιγίδα *ee* kate-**yee**dha

straight: straight on κατευθείαν katef-**thee**-an

straw *(for drinking)* το καλαμάκι *to* kala-**ma**kee

strawberry η φράουλα *ee* **fra**-oola

street ο δρόμος *o* **dhro**mos

street plan ο οδικός χάρτης *o* odhee-**kos** khar**tees**

string ο σπάγγος *o* **span**gos

striped ριγωτός reegho-**tos**

strong δυνατός dheena-**tos**

stuck *(jammed)* κολλημένος kolee-**me**nos

student ο φοιτητής/η φοιτήτρια *o* feetee-**tees**/ee fee-**tee**tree-a

stung: I've been stung κάτι μ' έχει κεντρίσει katee **me**khee ken-**dree**see

suddenly ξαφνικά ksaf-nee**ka**

suede το καστόρι *to* kas**to**ree

sugar η ζάχαρη *ee* **za**kharee

suit *(man's)* το κοστούμι *to* ko-**stoo**mee || *(woman's)* το ταγιέρ *to* ta**yer**

suitcase η βαλίτσα *ee* va**leet**-sa

summer το καλοκαίρι *to* kalo-**ke**ree

sun ο ήλιος *o* **ee**lee-os

sunbathe κάνω ηλιοθεραπεία **ka**no eelee-othe-ra**pee**-a

sunburn *(painful)* το κάψιμο από τον ήλιο *to* **kap**-seemo a**po** ton **ee**lee-o

sunglasses τα γιαλιά του ήλιου *ta* yalee-**a** too **ee**lee-oo

sunny *(weather)* ηλιόλουστος eelee**o**loostos

sunshade η ομπρέλα *ee* om**bre**la

sunstroke η ηλίαση *ee* ee**lee**-asee

suntan το μαύρισμα από τον ήλιο *to* **mav**-reesma a**po** ton **ee**lee-o

suntan lotion το λάδι για τον ήλιο *to* **la**dhee ya ton **ee**lee-o

supermarket το σούπερ-μάρκετ *to* supermarket

supper το δείπνο *to* **dheep**no

supplement το συμπλήρωμα *to* seem**blee**-roma

sure βέβαιος **ve**-ve-os

surface mail απλό ταχυδρομείο a**plo** takheedhromee-o

surfboard το σέρφπορντ *to* surfboard

surfing το σέρφινγκ *to* surfing

surname το επώνυμο *to* e**po**-neemo

suspension η ανάρτηση *ee* anar-**tee**see

sweater το πουλόβερ *to* poo**lo**ver

sweet[1] *adj (taste)* γλυκός ghlee**kos**

sweet[2] *n* το γλυκό *to* ghlee**ko**

sweetener η γλυκαντική ουσία *ee* ghleekantee**kee** oo**see**-a

swim κολυμπώ koleem-**bo**

swimming pool η πισίνα *ee* pee-**see**na

swimsuit το μαγιό *to* ma-**yo**

switch ο διακόπτης *o* dhee-a**kop**tees

switch on ανάβω a**na**vo

switch off σβήνω **svee**no

synagogue η συναγωγή *ee* seenagho-**yee**

table το τραπέζι *to* tra-**pe**zee

tablecloth το τραπεζομάντηλο *to* trapezo-**man**deelo

tablespoon το κουτάλι *to koo-ta-lee*

tablet το χάπι *to kha-pee*

table tennis το πινγκ πονγκ *to peeng pong*

take παίρνω *perno*

talc το ταλκ *to talk*

talk μιλώ *meelo*

tall ψηλός *pseelos*

tampons τα ταμπόν *ta tambon*

tap η βρύση *ee vreesee*

tape η ταινία *ee tenee-a*

tape recorder το μαγνητόφωνο *to maghnee-tofono*

taste¹ *vb* δοκιμάζω *dhokee-mazo*

taste² *n* η γεύση *ee yefsee*

tax ο φόρος *o foros*

taxi το ταξί *to taksee*

taxi rank η πιάτσα *ee pee-atsa*

tea το τσάι *to tsa-ee*

tea bag το σακκουλάκι *to sakoo-lakee*

teach διδάσκω *dhee-dhasko*

teacher ο δάσκαλος/η δασκάλα *o dhaska-los/ee dhaskala*

teapot η τσαγιέρα *ee tsa-yera*

teaspoon το κουτουλάκι *to koo-talakee*

teat η ρώγα *ee rogha*

teeshirt το μπλουζάκι *to bloozakee*

teeth τα δόντια *ta dhondee-a*

telegram το τηλεγράφημα *to teele-ghrafeema*

telephone το τηλέφωνο *to teele-fono*

telephone box ο τηλεφωνικός θάλαμος *o teele-fonee-kos thala-mos*

telephone call το τηλεφώνημα *to teele-foneema*

telephone directory ο τηλεφωνικός κατάλογος *o teele-fonee-kos kata-loghos*

television η τηλεόραση *ee teele-orasee*

telex το τέλεξ *to telex*

tell λέγω *legho* || (story) διηγούμαι *dhee-eeghoo-me*

temperature η θερμοκρασία *ee thermo-krasee-a* || **to have a temperature** έχω πυρετό *ekho pee-reto*

temporary προσωρινός *proso-reenos*

tennis το τέννις *to tenees*

tennis court το γήπεδο του τέννις *to yee-pedho too tenees*

tennis racket η ρακέτα του τέννις *ee ra-keta too tenees*

tent η σκηνή *ee skeenee*

tent peg ο πάσσαλος της σκηνής *o pasa-los tees skeenees*

terminus το τέρμα *to terma*

terrace η ταράτσα *ee taratsa*

than από *apo*

thank you ευχαριστώ *ef-kharee-sto*

that εκείνος *ekee-nos* || **that book** εκείνο το βιβλίο *ekee-no to veevlee-o* || **that one** εκείνο *ekee-no*

thaw: it's thawing λειώνει *lee-onee*

theatre το θέατρο *to the-atro*

then τότε *tote*

there εκεί *ekee* || **there is/there are** υπάρχει/υπάρχουν *ee-parkhee/ee-parkhoon*

thermometer το θερμόμετρο *to thermo-metro*

these αυτοί/αυτές/αυτά

aftee/aftes/afta ‖ **these books** αυτά τα βιβλία *afta ta veevlee-a*

they *see* GRAMMAR

thief ο κλέφτης *o kleftees*

thing το πράγμα *to praghma*

third τρίτος *treetos*

thirsty: I'm thirsty διψώ *dheepso*

this αυτός *aftos* ‖ **this book** αυτό το βιβλίο *afto to veevlee-o* ‖ **this one** αυτό *afto*

those εκείνοι *ekee-nee* ‖ **those books** εκείνα τα βιβλία *ekee-na ta veevlee-a*

thread η κλωστή *ee klostee*

throat ο λαιμός *o lemos*

throat lozenges οι παστίλιες του λαιμού *ee pasteelee-es too lemoo*

through διαμέσου *dhee-amesoo*

thunderstorm η θύελλα *ee theela*

ticket το εισιτήριο *to eesee-teeree-o*

ticket collector ο ελεγκτής *o eleng-tees*

ticket office η θυρίδα *ee thee-reedha*

tide η παλίρροια *ee paleeree-a*

tie η γραβάτα *ee ghra-vata*

tights το καλσόν *to kalson*

till[1] *n* το ταμείο *to tamee-o*

till[2] *(until)* μέχρι *mekhree*

time *(by the clock)* η ώρα *ee ora* ‖ *(duration)* ο καιρός *o keros* ‖ **what time is it?** τι ώρα είναι; *tee ora ee-ne?*

timetable το δρομολόγιο *to dhromo-loyee-o*

tin η κονσέρβα *ee kon-serva*

tinfoil το ασημόχαρτο *to aseemo-kharto*

tin-opener το ανοιχτήρι για κονσέρβες *to aneekh-teeree ya kon-ser-ves*

tip *(to waiter, etc)* το πουρμπουάρ *to poorboo-ar*

tipped *(cigarettes)* με φίλτρο *me feeltro*

tired κουρασμένος *kooras-menos*

tissue το χαρτομάντηλο *to kharto-mandeelo*

to σε *se* ‖ **to Greece** στην Ελλάδα *steen eladha*

toast η φρυγανιά *ee freeghanee-a*

tobacco ο καπνός *o kapnos*

tobacconist's το καπνοπωλείο *to kapno-polee-o*

today σήμερα *see-mera*

together μαζί *mazee*

toilet η τουαλέτα *ee too-aleta* ‖ **toilet paper** το χαρτί υγείας *to khartee eeyee-as*

toll τα διόδια *ta dhee-odhee-a*

tomato η ντομάτα *ee domata*

tomato juice ο χυμός ντομάτας *o kheemos domatas*

tomorrow αύριο *avree-o*

tongue η γλώσσα *ee glosa*

tonic water το τόνικ *to toneek*

tonight απόψε *apop-se*

too *(also)* επίσης *epee-sees* ‖ *(too much)* πολύ *polee*

tooth το δόντι *to dhondee*

toothache ο πονόδοντος *o pono-dhondos*

toothbrush το βουρτσάκι για τα δόντια *to voort-sakee ya ta dhondee-a*

toothpaste η οδοντόκρεμα *ee odhon-dokrema*

top το πάνω μέρος *to pano meros*
|| (of mountain) η κορυφή *ee koree-fee*

torch ο φακός *o fakos*

torn σχισμένος *skhees-menos*

total το σύνολο *to see-nolo*

tough (of meat) σκληρός *skleros*

tour η περιοδεία *ee peree-odhee-a*

tourist ο τουρίστας/η τουρίστρια *o too-reestas/ee too-reestree-a*

tourist office το τουριστικό γραφείο *to tooree-steeko ghrafee-o*

tourist ticket το τουριστικό εισιτήριο *to tooree-steeko eesee-teeree-o*

tow ρυμουλκώ *reemool-ko*

towel η πετσέτα *ee pet-seta*

town η πόλη *ee polee*

town centre το κέντρο της πόλης *to kendro tees polees*

town plan ο χάρτης της πόλης *o khartees tees polees*

towrope το σχοινί ρυμούλκησης *to skheenee reemool-keesees*

toy το παιχνίδι *to pegh-needhee*

traditional παραδοσιακός *para-dhosee-akos*

traffic η κυκλοφορία *ee keeklo-foree-a*

trailer το ρυμουλκούμενο όχημα *to reemool-koomeno okhee-ma*

train το τραίνο *to treno*

training shoes παπούτσια γυμναστικής *papootseea gheemnasteekees*

tram το τραμ *to tram*

translate μεταφράζω *meta-frazo*

translation η μετάφραση *ee meta-frasee*

travel ταξιδεύω *taksee-dhevo*

travel agent ο ταξιδιωτικός πράκτορας *o takseedhee-oteekos prak-toras*

traveller's cheque το τράβελερς-τσεκ *to traveller's cheque*

tray ο δίσκος *o dheeskos*

tree το δέντρο *to dhendro*

trim (hair) το κόψιμο *to kop-seemo*

trip η εκδρομή *ee ek-dhromee*

trolley bus το τρόλλεϋ *to tro-le-ee*

trouble ο μπελάς *o belas*

trousers το παντελόνι *to pande-lonee*

true αληθινός *alee-theenos*

trunk το μπαούλο *to ba-oolo*

trunks το μαγιό *to ma-yo*

try προσπαθώ *pros-patho*

try on δοκιμάζω *dhokee-mazo*

T-shirt Τ σερτ *T-shirt*

tuna ο τόννος *o tonos*

tunnel η σήραγγα *ee see-ranga*

turkey η γαλοπούλα *ee ghalo-poola*

turn¹ n η σειρά *ee seera*

turn² vb γυρίζω *yee-reezo*

turnip η ρέβα *ee reva*

turn off (on a journey) στρίβω *streevo* || (radio, etc) κλείνω *kleeno* || (engine, light) σβήνω *sveeno*

turn on (radio, etc) ανοίγω *anee-gho* || (engine, light) ανάβω *anavo*

TV η τηλεόραση *ee teele-orasee*

tweezers το τσιμπίδι *to tseem-beedhee*

twice δυο φορές *dhee-o fo-res*

twin ο δίδυμος *o dhee-dheemos* || **twin-bedded** το δίκλινο δωμάτιο *to dhee-kleeno dhomatee-o*

typical χαρακτηριστικός *kharak-teeree-steekos*

tyre το λάστιχο *to lastee-kho*

tyre pressure η πίεση στα λάστιχα *ee pee-esee sta lastee-kha*

umbrella η ομπρέλα *ee ombrela*

uncomfortable όχι άνετο *okhee a-neto*

unconscious αναίσθητος *a-nes-theetos*

under κάτω από *kato apo*

underground *(railway)* ο υπόγειος σιδηρόδρομος *o eepoyee-os seedhee-rodhromos*

underpass η υπόγεια διάβαση *ee eepoyee-a dhee-avasee*

understand καταλαβαίνω *kata-laveno*

underwear τα εσώρουχα *ta esorookha*

United States οι Ηνωμένες Πολιτείες *ee eeno-me-nes poleetee-es*

university το πανεπιστήμιο *to panepee-steemee-o*

unpack *(case)* αδειάζω *adhee-azo*

up *(out of bed)* σηκωμένος *seeko-menos* || **go up** ανεβαίνω *a-ne-veno*

upstairs πάνω *pano*

urgently επειγόντως *epee-ghondos*

use χρησιμοποιώ *khreesee-mopee-o*

useful χρήσιμος *khreesee-mos*

usual συνηθισμένος *seenee-theesmenos*

usually συνήθως *see-neethos*

vacancy το διαθέσιμο δωμάτιο *to dhee-athe-seemo dhomatee-o*

vacuum cleaner η ηλεκτρική σκούπα *ee eelek-treekee skoopa*

valid έγκυρος *engee-ros*

valley η κοιλάδα *ee kee-ladha*

valuable πολύτιμος *polee-teemos*

valuables τα πολύτιμα αντικείμενα *ta poleeteema anteekeemena*

value η αξία *ee aksee-a*

van το φορτηγάκι *to fortee-ghakee*

vase το βάζο *to vazo*

VAT ο ΦΠΑ *o fee-pee-a*

veal το μοσχάρι *to mos-kharee*

vegetables τα λαχανικά *ta lakha-neeka*

vegetarian ο χορτοφάγος *o khorto-faghos*

ventilator ο εξαεριστήρας *o eksa-eree-steeras*

vermouth το βερμούτ *to vermoot*

very πολύ *polee*

vest η φανέλα *ee fanela*

via μέσω *meso*

video το βίντεο *to video*

view η θέα *ee the-a*

villa *(by the sea)* η έπαυλη *ee epav-lee*

village το χωριό *to khoree-o*

vinegar το ξύδι *to kseedhee*

visa η θεώρηση *ee the-o-reesee*

visit επισκέπτομαι *epeeskeptome*

vitamin η βιταμίνη *ee veeta-meenee*

vodka η βότκα *ee votka*

voltage η τάση *ee tasee*

waist η μέση *ee mesee*

wait (for) περιμένω *peree-meno*

waiter το γκαρσόνι *to gar-sonee*

waiting room η αίθουσα αναμονής *ee ethoo-sa ana-monees*

waitress η σερβιτόρα *ee servee-tora*

Wales η Ουαλία *ee oo-alee-a*

walk¹ n ο περίπατος *o peree-patos*

walk² vb περπατώ *per-pato*

wallet το πορτοφόλι *to porto-folee*

walnut το καρύδι *to ka-reedhee*

want θέλω *thelo*

warm ζεστός *zestos*

warning triangle το τρίγωνο αυτοκινήτου *to tree-ghono afto-keeneetoo*

wash (clothes) πλένω *pleno* || (oneself) πλένομαι *pleno-me*

washbasin η λεκάνη *ee le-kanee*

washing machine το πλυντήριο *to pleendeeree-o*

washing powder σκόνη πλυσίματος *skonee pleeseematos*

washing-up liquid υγρό για τα πιάτα *eeghro ya ta pee-ata*

wasp η σφήκα *ee sfeeka*

waste bin το δοχείο *to dhokhee-o*

watch¹ n το ρολόι *to rolo-ee*

watch² vb (TV) βλέπω *vlepo* || (someone's luggage) προσέχω *pro-sekho*

water το νερό *to nero*

waterfall ο καταρράκτης *o kata-raktees*

water heater ο θερμοσίφωνας *o thermo-seefonas*

water-skiing το θαλάσσιο σκι *to thalasee-o skee*

watermelon το καρπούζι *to kar-poozee*

waterproof αδιάβροχος *adhee-avrokhos*

wave (on sea) το κύμα *to keema*

wax το κερί *to keree*

way (method) ο τρόπος *o tropos* || **this/that way** απ' εδώ/απ' εκεί *apedho/apekee*

we εμείς *emees*

weak αδύνατος *adhee-natos*

wear φορώ *foro*

weather ο καιρός *o keros*

wedding ο γάμος *o ghamos*

week η εβδομάδα *ee ev-dhomadha*

weekday η καθημερινή *ee kathee-mereenee*

weekend το σαββατοκύριακο *to savato-keeree-ako*

weekly (rate, etc) εβδομαδιαίος *ev-dhomadhee-e-os*

weight το βάρος *to varos*

welcome καλώς ήλθατε *kalos eeltha-te*

well (healthy) υγιής *eeyee-ees* || **well done** (steak) καλοψημένος *kalopseemenos*

Welsh Ουαλός/Ουαλή *oo-alos/oo-alee*

west η δύση *ee dheesee*

wet (damp) βρεγμένος *vreghmenos* || (weather) βροχερός *vro-kheros*

wetsuit η στολή για υποβρύχιο ψάρεμα *ee stolee ya eepo-vreekhee-o psa-rema*

what τι *tee* || **what is it?** τι είναι; *tee ee-ne?* || **what book?** ποιο βιβλίο; *pee-o veevlee-o?*

wheel ο τροχός *o trokhos*

wheelchair η αναπηρική καρέκλα *ee ana-peereekee ka-rekla*

when? όταν; *otan?*

where? πού; *poo?*

which? ποιος; *pee-os?* || **which is it?** ποιο είναι; *pee-o ee-ne?*

while ενώ *eno*

whipped *(cream)* η χτυπημένη κρέμα *ee khteepeemenee krema*

whisky το ουίσκυ *to oo-eeskee*

white άσπρος *aspros*

who ποιος *pee-os*

whole όλος *olos*

wholemeal bread μαύρο ψωμί *mavro psomee*

whose: whose is it? ποιου είναι; *pee-oo ee-ne?*

why? γιατί; *yatee?*

wide πλατύς *platees*

wife η σύζυγος *ee seezee-ghos*

window το παράθυρο *to para-theero*

windscreen το παρμπρίζ *to par-breez*

windsurfing το γουίντσερφινγκ *to windsurfing*

wine το κρασί *to krasee*

wine list ο κατάλογος των κρασιών *o kata-loghos ton krasee-on*

winter ο χειμώνας *o khee-monas*

with με *me*

without χωρίς *khorees*

woman η γυναίκα *ee yee-neka*

wood το ξύλο *to kseelo*

wool το μαλλί *to malee*

work *(person)* δουλεύω *dhoo-levo* || *(machine)* λειτουργώ *leetoor-gho*

worried ανήσυχος *anee-seekhos*

worse χειρότερος *kheero-teros*

worth: 2000 drachmas worth of petrol 2000 δραχμές βενζίνη *thee-o kheelee-adhes dhrakhmes venzeenee* || **it's worth 2000 drachmas** αξίζει 2000 δραχμές *akseezee thee-o kheelee-adhes dhrakhmes*

wrap (up) τυλίγω *tee-leegho*

wrapping paper το χαρτί περιτυλίγματος *to khartee peree-teeleegh-matos*

write γράφω *ghrafo*

writing paper το χαρτί αλληλογραφίας *to khartee aleelo-ghrafee-as*

wrong λάθος *lathos* || **you're wrong** κάνετε λάθος *ka-ne-te lathos*

yacht το γιωτ *to yacht*

year ο χρόνος *o khronos*

yellow κίτρινος *keetree-nos*

yes ναι *ne*

yesterday χθες *khthes*

yet ακόμα *akoma* || **not yet** όχι ακόμα *okhee akoma*

yoghurt το γιαούρτι *to ya-oortee*

you *(sing./pl.)* εσύ/εσείς *esee/e-sees*

young νέος *ne-os*

zero μηδέν *mee-dhen*

zip το φερμουάρ *to fermoo-ar*

zoo ο ζωολογικός κήπος *o zo-olo-yeekos keepos*

άγαλμα (το) statue
αγάπη (η) love
αγαπώ to love
αγγείο (το) vessel; urn
αγγειοπλαστική (η) pottery
αγγελία (η) announcement
άγγελος (ο) angel
Αγγλία (η) England
αγγλικός/ή/ό English *(thing)*
Άγγλος/ίδα (ο/η) Englishman/-woman
αγγούρι (το) cucumber
αγγουροντομάτα (η) cucumber and tomato salad
άγιος/α/ο holy; saint || Άγιον Όρος (το) the Holy
  Mountain || Άγιος Παντελεήμων sweet white wine
  from Cyprus
αγκινάρα (η) artichoke
αγκίστρι (το) fishing hook
άγκυρα (η) anchor
αγορά (η) agora; market
αγοράζω to buy
αγορανομικός έλεγχος price control
αγοραστής (ο) buyer
αγόρι young boy
άδεια (η) permit; licence || άδεια οδηγήσεως driving
  licence || άδεια φωτογραφήσεως permit to take
  photographs
άδειος/α/ο empty
αδελφή (η) sister
αδελφός (ο) brother
Άδης (ο) Hades
αδιάβροχο (το) raincoat
αδιέξοδος (ο) cul-de-sac; no through road
αδίκημα (το) offence
αδικία (η) injustice
αέρας (ο) wind
αερογραμμές (οι) airways || Βρετανικές Αερογραμμές
  British Airways || Ολυμπιακές Αερογραμμές Olympic

Α	α	A
Β	β	V
Γ	γ	G
Δ	δ	D
Ε	ε	E
Ζ	ζ	Z
Η	η	I
Θ	θ	Th
Ι	ι	I
Κ	κ	K
Λ	λ	L
Μ	μ	M
Ν	ν	N
Ξ	ξ	X
Ο	ο	O
Π	π	P
Ρ	ρ	R
Σ	σ,ς	S
Τ	τ	T
Υ	υ	I
Φ	φ	F
Χ	χ	H
Ψ	ψ	Ps
Ω	ω	O

Airways ‖ **Κυπριακές Αερογραμμές** Cyprus Airways

αεροδρόμιο (το) airport

αερολιμένας/αερολιμήν (ο) airport

αεροπλάνο (το) aeroplane

αεροπορία (η) air force

αεροπορικό εισιτήριο (το) air ticket

αεροπορική αλληλογραφία (η) air mail

αεροπορικώς by air

αεροσκάφος (το) aircraft

αζήτητος/η/ο unclaimed

Αθήνα (η) Athens

αθλητικό κέντρο sports centre

αθλητισμός (ο) sports

'Άθως Athos, the Holy Mountain; Athos, a dry white wine

Αιγαίο (το) the Aegean Sea

αίθουσα (η) room ‖ **αίθουσα αναμονής** waiting room ‖ **αίθουσα αναχωρήσεων** departure lounge

αίμα (το) blood

αίτημα (το) demand

αίτηση (η) application

ακάθαρτος/η/ο dirty

ακουστικά (τα) earphones ‖ **ακουστικά βαρυκοΐας** hearing aids

ακουστικό (το) receiver *(telephone)*

ακούω to hear

άκρη (η) edge

Ακρόπολη/ις (η) the Acropolis

ακτή (η) beach; shore

ακτινογραφία (η) X-ray

ακυρώνω to cancel

αλάτι (το) salt

αλεύρι (το) flour

αλιεία (η) fishing ‖ **είδη αλιείας** fishing tackle

αλλαγή (η) change ‖ **δεν γίνονται αλλαγές** goods cannot be exchanged ‖ **δεν αλλάζονται** goods will not be exchanged

Α	α	A
Β	β	V
Γ	γ	G
Δ	δ	D
Ε	ε	E
Ζ	ζ	Z
Η	η	I
Θ	θ	Th
Ι	ι	I
Κ	κ	K
Λ	λ	L
Μ	μ	M
Ν	ν	N
Ξ	ξ	X
Ο	ο	O
Π	π	P
Ρ	ρ	R
Σ	σ,ς	S
Τ	τ	T
Υ	υ	I
Φ	φ	F
Χ	χ	H
Ψ	ψ	Ps
Ω	ω	O

αλληλογραφία (η) correspondence
αλληλογραφώ to correspond
αλλοδαπός/ή foreign national || **αστυνομία αλλοδαπών** immigration police
αλμυρός/ή/ό salty
αλτ! stop!
αλυσίδα (η) chain
αμάξωμα (το) body (of car)
άμβωνας (ο) pulpit
αμερικάνικος/η/ο American (thing)
Αμερικανός/ίδα American (man/woman)
Αμερική (η) America
αμέσως at once
αμήν amen
άμμος (η) sand
αμμουδιά (η) sandy beach
αμοιβή (η) reward
αμπέλι (το) vineyard; vine
αμύγδαλο (το) almond
αμφιθέατρο (το) amphitheatre
αμφορέας (ο) jar
αν if
αναβολή (η) delay
ανάβω to switch on
αναγγελία (η) announcement
ανάγλυφο (το) relief sculpture
αναζήτηση (η) search || **αναζήτηση αποσκευών** left-luggage (office)
ανάκριση (η) interrogation
ανάκτορα (τα) palace
αναμονή (η) waiting || **αίθουσα αναμονής** waiting room
ανανάς (ο) pineapple
ανανεώνω to renew
ανάπηρος/η/ο handicapped; disabled
αναπληρώνω to replace
αναπτήρας (ο) cigarette lighter
ανασκαφή (η) excavation

A	α	A
B	β	V
Γ	γ	G
Δ	δ	D
E	ε	E
Z	ζ	Z
H	η	I
Θ	θ	Th
I	ι	I
K	κ	K
Λ	λ	L
M	μ	M
N	ν	N
Ξ	ξ	X
O	o	O
Π	π	P
P	ρ	R
Σ	σ,ς	S
T	τ	T
Υ	υ	I
Φ	φ	F
X	χ	H
Ψ	ψ	Ps
Ω	ω	O

ανατολή (η) east

αναχώρηση (η) departure || αναχωρήσεις departures || αίθουσα αναχωρήσεων departure lounge

αναψυκτήριο (το) refreshments

αναψυκτικό (το) soft drink

αναψυχή (η) recreation

άνδρας (ο) man

ανδρική μόδα men's fashions

Ανδρών Men (toilets)

ανελκυστήρας (ο) lift; elevator

ανεμιστήρας (ο) fan

άνθη (τα) flowers

ανθοπωλείο (το) florist's

άνθρωπος (ο) man

ανοικτός/ή/ό open

άνοιξη (η) spring

ανταλλαγή (η) exchange

ανταλλακτικά (τα) spare parts || γνήσια ανταλλακτικά genuine spare parts

αντιβιοτικά (τα) antibiotics

αντίγραφο (το) copy; reproduction

αντίκες (οι) antiques

αντικλεπτικά (τα) anti-theft devices

αντίο goodbye

αντιπηκτικό (το) antifreeze

αντιπρόσωπος (ο) representative

αντλία (η) pump || αντλία βενζίνης petrol pump

αντρόγυνο (το) couple

ανώμαλος/η/ο uneven || ανωμαλία οδοστρώματος bad or uneven road surface

αξεσουάρ (τα) accessories || αξεσουάρ αυτοκινήτων car accessories

αξία (η) value || αξία διαδρομής fare

αξιοθέατα (τα) the sights

απαγορεύω to forbid || απαγορεύεται η αναμονή no waiting || απαγορεύεται η διάβαση keep off || απαγορεύεται η είσοδος no entry || απαγορεύεται το

Α	α	A
Β	β	V
Γ	γ	G
Δ	δ	D
Ε	ε	E
Ζ	ζ	Z
Η	η	I
Θ	θ	Th
Ι	ι	I
Κ	κ	K
Λ	λ	L
Μ	μ	M
Ν	ν	N
Ξ	ξ	X
Ο	ο	O
Π	π	P
Ρ	ρ	R
Σ	σ,ς	S
Τ	τ	T
Υ	υ	I
Φ	φ	F
Χ	χ	H
Ψ	ψ	Ps
Ω	ω	O

κάπνισμα no smoking || απαγορεύεται το προσπέρασμα
no overtaking || απαγορεύεται η στάθμευση no parking
|| απαγορεύεται η τοιχοκόλληση no bills ||
απαγορεύεται η τοποθέτηση σκουπιδιών no dumping (of
rubbish) || απαγορεύονται τα σκυλιά no dogs ||
απαγορεύεται η φωτογράφηση no photography

απαίτηση (η) claim

απαλλαγή ευθύνης collision damage waiver (insurance)

Απελία a dry white wine

απεργία (η) strike

από from

απογείωση (η) takeoff

απόγευμα (το) afternoon

απόδειξη (η) receipt

αποθήκη (η) warehouse

αποκλειστικός/ή/ό exclusive || **αποκλειστικός**
αντιπρόσωπος sole representative

απόκριες (οι) carnival

αποσκευές (οι) luggage || **αναζήτηση αποσκευών** left-
luggage (office)

απόχη (η) fishing net; butterfly net

απόψε tonight

Απρίλιος (ο) April

αργότερα later

αρέσω to please || **μου αρέσει** I like

αριθμός (ο) number || **αριθμός διαβατηρίου** passport
number || **αριθμός πτήσεως** flight number

αριστερά left (side)

αρνί (το) lamb

αρρώστια (η) illness

άρρωστος/η/ο ill || **άρρωστος/η** patient

αρτοποιία (η) bakery

αρχαιολογικός χώρος archaeological site

αρχαιολόγος (ο/η) archaeologist

αρχαίος/α/ο ancient

αρχή (η) beginning; authority

αρχιεπισκοπή (η) archbishopric

Α	α	A
Β	β	V
Γ	γ	G
Δ	δ	D
Ε	ε	E
Ζ	ζ	Z
Η	η	I
Θ	θ	Th
Ι	ι	I
Κ	κ	K
Λ	λ	L
Μ	μ	M
Ν	ν	N
Ξ	ξ	X
Ο	ο	O
Π	π	P
Ρ	ρ	R
Σ	σ,ς	S
Τ	τ	T
Υ	υ	I
Φ	φ	F
Χ	χ	H
Ψ	ψ	Ps
Ω	ω	O

αρχιεπίσκοπος (ο) archbishop
αρχίζω to begin
άρωμα (το) perfume
ασανσέρ (το) lift; elevator
ασθενής (ο/η) patient
άσθμα (το) asthma
άσκοπος/η/ο improper; lacking in purpose || άσκοπη χρήση improper use
ασπιρίνη (η) aspirin
άσπρος/η/ο white
αστακός (ο) lobster
αστικός νομισματοδέκτης coin-operated telephone for local calls
αστυνομία (η) police || αστυνομία αλλοδαπών immigration police
αστυνομική διάταξη police notice
αστυνομικός σταθμός police station
αστυφύλακας (ο) town policeman
ασφάλεια (η) insurance; fuse || ασφάλεια έναντι κλοπής insurance against theft || ασφάλεια έναντι πυρκαϊάς insurance against fire || ασφάλεια έναντι τρίτων third-party insurance || ασφάλεια ζωής life insurance
ασφάλιση (η) insurance || κοινωνικές ασφαλίσεις national insurance || ασφάλιση οδηγού και επιβαινόντων personal accident insurance || πλήρης ασφάλιση comprehensive insurance
ατμοπλοϊκό εισιτήριο boat ticket
ατύχημα (το) accident
αυγό (το) egg || αυγό βραστό boiled egg || αυγό μελάτο soft boiled egg || αυγό ποσέ poached egg || αυγό τηγανιτό fried egg || αυγά ημέρας newly-laid eggs
αυγολέμονο (το) soup containing rice, chicken stock, egg and lemon
Αύγουστος (ο) August
αυτοκίνητο (το) car || ενοικιάσεις αυτοκινήτων car hire || Ελληνική Λέσχη Αυτοκινήτου και Περιηγήσεων The Automobile and Touring Club of Greece || στάθμευση αυτοκινήτων car parking || συνεργείο αυτοκινήτων car repairs

A	α	A
B	β	V
Γ	γ	G
Δ	δ	D
E	ε	E
Z	ζ	Z
H	η	I
Θ	θ	Th
I	ι	I
K	κ	K
Λ	λ	L
M	μ	M
N	ν	N
Ξ	ξ	X
O	ο	O
Π	π	P
P	ρ	R
Σ	σ,ς	S
T	τ	T
Υ	υ	I
Φ	φ	F
X	χ	H
Ψ	ψ	Ps
Ω	ω	O

αυτοκινητόδρομος (ο) motorway
αυτόματος/η/ο automatic || **αυτόματη μετάδοση** automatic transmission
αυτοψωνίζετε self-service
άφιξη (η) arrival || **αφίξεις** arrivals || **δελτίο αφίξεως** arrival card
αφορολόγητα (τα) duty-free goods
Αφροδίτη Aphrodite, a medium white wine from Cyprus
αχθοφόρος (ο) porter
αχλάδι (το) pear
άχρηστα (τα) waste
αψίδα (η) arch

βαγόνι (το) carriage *(train)*
βαλβίδα (η) valve
βαλίτσα (η) suitcase
βαμβακερός/ή/ό (made of) cotton
βαρέλι (το) barrel || **μπύρα από βαρέλι** draught beer
βάρκα (η) boat
βάρος (το) weight
βαφή (η) paint; dye
βγάζω to take off
βγαίνω to go out
βελόνα (η) needle
βενζίνη (η) petrol
βήχας (ο) cough
βιβλίο (το) book
βιβλιοθήκη (η) bookcase; library || **Δημοτική Βιβλιοθήκη** Public Library || **Κεντρική Βιβλιοθήκη** Central Library
βιβλιοπωλείο (το) bookshop
Βίβλος (η) the Bible
βιταμίνη (η) vitamin
βιτρίνα (η) shop window
βόδι (το) ox
βοδινό κρέας beef
βοήθεια (η) help || **οδική βοήθεια** breakdown service ||

A	α	A
B	β	V
Γ	γ	G
Δ	δ	D
E	ε	E
Z	ζ	Z
H	η	I
Θ	θ	Th
I	ι	I
K	κ	K
Λ	λ	L
M	μ	M
N	ν	N
Ξ	ξ	X
O	ο	O
Π	π	P
P	ρ	R
Σ	σ,ς	S
T	τ	T
Υ	υ	I
Φ	φ	F
X	χ	H
Ψ	ψ	Ps
Ω	ω	O

πρώτες βοήθειες first aid
βόμβα (η) bomb
βομβητής (ο) buzzer
βορράς (ο) north
βουλή (η) parliament
βουνό (το) mountain
βούρτσα (η) brush
βούτυρος (ο) butter
βράδυ (το) evening
Βρετανία (η) Britain
βρετανικος/ή/ό British *(thing)* || Βρετανικές
  Αερογραμμές British Airways
Βρετανός/ίδα British *(man/woman)*
βροχερός/ή/ό rainy || βροχερός καιρός wet weather
βροχή (η) rain
βρύση (η) tap; fountain

γάιδαρος (ο) donkey
γάλα (το) milk
γαλάζιος/α/ο blue
γαλακτοπωλείο (το) dairy products
Γαλλία (η) France
γαλλικός/ή/ό French *(thing)*
Γάλλος/ίδα French *(man/woman)*
γαλοπούλα (η) turkey
γάμος (ο) wedding; marriage
γαρίδα (η) shrimp
γεια σου hello; goodbye
γεμάτος/η/ο full
γενέθλια (τα) birthday
γενικός/ή/ό general || Γενικό Νοσοκομείο General
  Hospital
γέννηση (η) birth
Γερμανία (η) Germany
γερμανικός/ή/ό German *(thing)*
Γερμανός/ίδα German *(man/woman)*

Α	α	A
Β	β	V
Γ	γ	G
Δ	δ	D
Ε	ε	E
Ζ	ζ	Z
Η	η	I
Θ	θ	Th
Ι	ι	I
Κ	κ	K
Λ	λ	L
Μ	μ	M
Ν	ν	N
Ξ	ξ	X
Ο	ο	O
Π	π	P
Ρ	ρ	R
Σ	σ,ς	S
Τ	τ	T
Υ	υ	I
Φ	φ	F
Χ	χ	H
Ψ	ψ	Ps
Ω	ω	O

γεύμα (το) meal
γέφυρα (η) bridge
για for
γιαγιά (η) grandmother
γιαούρτι (το) yoghurt
γιασεμί (το) jasmine
γιατί why; because
γιατρός (ο/η) doctor
γίνομαι to become ‖ **γίνονται δεκτές πιστωτικές κάρτες** we accept credit cards
γιορτή (η) public holiday
γιωτ (το) yacht
γκάζι (το) accelerator (car); gas
γκαράζ (το) garage
γκαρσόν (το)/**γκαρσόνι** (το) waiter
γλυκός/ιά/ό sweet ‖ **γλυκό** (το)/**γλυκά** (τα) sweet pastries and cakes ‖ **γλυκά** (τα) patisserie ‖ **γλυκό ταψιού** pastries in syrup
γλύπτης (ο/η) sculptor
γλυπτική (η) sculpture
γλώσσα (η) tongue; language; sole (fish)
γονείς (οι) parents
γουίντσερφινγκ (το) windsurfing
γράμμα (το) letter ‖ **γράμμα επείγον** urgent or express letter ‖ **γράμμα συστημένο** registered letter
γραμμάριο (το) gramme
γραμματοκιβώτιο (το) letter box
γραμματόσημο (το) stamp ‖ **αυτόματος πωλητής γραμματοσήμων** automatic stamp dispenser
γραφείο (το) office; desk ‖ **Γραφείο Τουρισμού** Tourist Office
γρήγορα quickly
γρίππη (η) influenza
γυαλί (το) glass ‖ **γυαλιά** (τα) glasses ‖ **γυαλιά του ήλιου** sunglasses
γυιος (ο) son
γυναίκα (η) woman ‖ **γυναικών** Ladies' (toilets)

Α	α	A
Β	β	V
Γ	γ	G
Δ	δ	D
Ε	ε	E
Ζ	ζ	Z
Η	η	I
Θ	θ	Th
Ι	ι	I
Κ	κ	K
Λ	λ	L
Μ	μ	M
Ν	ν	N
Ξ	ξ	X
Ο	ο	O
Π	π	P
Ρ	ρ	R
Σ	σ,ς	S
Τ	τ	T
Υ	υ	I
Φ	φ	F
Χ	χ	H
Ψ	ψ	Ps
Ω	ω	O

γύρος (ο) doner kebab
γύρω round; about
γωνία (η) corner

δακτυλίδι (το) ring *(for finger)*
δακτύλιος (ο) ring; circle
δαμάσκηνο (το) plum
δαντέλα (η) lace
δασκάλα (η) teacher *(female)*
δάσκαλος (ο) teacher *(male)*
δασμός (ο) duty; tax
δάσος (το) forest
δείπνο (το) dinner
δέκα ten
Δεκέμβριος (ο) December
δελτίο (το) card; coupon || **δελτίο αφίξεως** arrival card || **δελτίο λιανικής πωλήσεως** bill for retail sale
δελφίνι (το) dolphin || **ιπτάμενο δελφίνι** hydrofoil
Δελφοί (οι) Delphi
δέμα (το) parcel
Δεμέστικα a dry white or red wine
δεν not || **δεν γίνονται αλλαγές** goods cannot be exchanged || **δεν δίνει ρέστα** no change given
δεξιά right *(side)*
δέρμα (το) skin; leather
δεσποινίσίδα (η) Miss
Δευτέρα (η) Monday
δεύτερος/η/ο second
δήλωση (η) announcement; statement || **δήλωση συναλλάγματος** currency declaration || **είδη προς δήλωση** goods to declare || **ουδέν προς δήλωση** nothing to declare
δημαρχείο (το) Town Hall
δημοκρατία (η) democracy
δημόσιος/α/ο public || **δημόσια έργα** public works; road works || **δημόσιος κήπος** public gardens
δημοτικός/ή/ό public || **Δημοτική Αγορά** (public)

Α	α	A
Β	β	V
Γ	γ	G
Δ	δ	D
Ε	ε	E
Ζ	ζ	Z
Η	η	I
Θ	θ	Th
Ι	ι	I
Κ	κ	K
Λ	λ	L
Μ	μ	M
Ν	ν	N
Ξ	ξ	X
Ο	ο	O
Π	π	P
Ρ	ρ	R
Σ	σ,ς	S
Τ	τ	T
Υ	υ	I
Φ	φ	F
Χ	χ	H
Ψ	ψ	Ps
Ω	ω	O

market || **Δημοτική Βιβλιοθήκη** Public Library

διάβαση πεζών pedestrian crossing || **υπόγεια διάβαση πεζών** (pedestrian) subway

διαβατήριο (το) passport || **αριθμός διαβατηρίου** passport number || **έλεγχος διαβατηρίων** passport control

διαβήτης (ο) diabetes

διαδρομή (η) route

δίαιτα (η) diet

διακεκριμένος/η/ο distinguished || **διακεκριμένη θέση** business class

διακοπές (οι) holidays

διάλειμμα (το) interval; break

διάλυση (η) closing down

διαμέρισμα (το) flat; apartment

διανυχτερεύει all-night *(chemist, bar, etc)*

διάρκεια (η) duration || **κατά τη διάρκεια της ημέρας** during the day

διασκέδαση (η) entertainment || **κέντρο διασκεδάσεως** nightclub

διατηρώ to preserve; to keep || **διατηρείτε την πόλη καθαρή** keep the town clean

διατροφή (η): πλήρης διατροφή full board

δίδραχμο (το) two-drachma piece

διεθνής/ής/ές international

διερμηνέας (ο/η) interpreter

διεύθυνση (η) address; management

διευθυντής (ο) manager; headmaster

δικαστήριο (το) court

δικηγόρος (ο) lawyer

διπλός/ή/ό double || **διπλό δωμάτιο** double room || **διπλό κρεββάτι** double bed

διπλότυπος λογαριασμός duplicate bill

δισκοθήκη (η) disco

δίσκος (ο) record

δίχτυ (το) net

διψώ to be thirsty

διώκω to persecute; **διώκεται ποινικώς** will be prosecuted

Α	α	A
Β	β	V
Γ	γ	G
Δ	δ	D
Ε	ε	E
Ζ	ζ	Z
Η	η	I
Θ	θ	Th
Ι	ι	I
Κ	κ	K
Λ	λ	L
Μ	μ	M
Ν	ν	N
Ξ	ξ	X
Ο	ο	O
Π	π	P
Ρ	ρ	R
Σ	σ,ς	S
Τ	τ	T
Υ	υ	I
Φ	φ	F
Χ	χ	H
Ψ	ψ	Ps
Ω	ω	O

δολλάριο (το) dollar

δόντι (το) tooth

δραχμή (η) drachma

δρομολόγιο (το) timetable; route || εξωτερικά δρομολόγια international routes || εσωτερικά δρομολόγια internal routes

δρόμος (ο) street; way

δύο two

δύση (η) west

δυσκοιλιότητα (η) constipation

δυστύχημα (το) accident

δυτικός/ή/ό western

Δωδεκάνησα (τα) the Dodecanese

δωμάτιο (το) room

δωρεάν free of charge

δώρο (το) present; gift

εβδομάδα (η) week

εγγραφή (η) registration

εγγύηση (η) deposit; guarantee

έγχρωμος/η/ο coloured || έγχρωμες φωτογραφίες colour photographs

εδώ here

εθνικός/ή/ό national || εθνικό θέατρο national theatre || εθνικοί οδοί national highways || εθνικός κήπος public garden || εθνικός ύμνος national anthem

έθνος (το) nation

ειδικός/ή/ό specialist || ειδικό τμήμα ... special department for ...

είδος (το) kind; sort || είδη goods || είδη αλιείας fishing tackle || είδη προς δήλωση goods to declare || είδη εξοχής camping equipment || είδη καπνιστού tobacconist || είδη κήπου garden centre || είδη υγιεινής bathrooms

εισιτήριο (το) ticket || εισιτήριο απλής διαδρομής single ticket || εισιτήριο μετ' επιστροφής return ticket || ατμοπλοϊκό εισιτήριο boat ticket || σιδηροδρομικό εισιτήριο rail ticket || φοιτητικό εισιτήριο student ticket

Α	α	A
Β	β	V
Γ	γ	G
Δ	δ	D
Ε	ε	E
Ζ	ζ	Z
Η	η	I
Θ	θ	Th
Ι	ι	I
Κ	κ	K
Λ	λ	L
Μ	μ	M
Ν	ν	N
Ξ	ξ	X
Ο	ο	O
Π	π	P
Ρ	ρ	R
Σ	σ,ς	S
Τ	τ	T
Υ	υ	I
Φ	φ	F
Χ	χ	H
Ψ	ψ	Ps
Ω	ω	O

είσοδος (η) entrance; entry

εισπράκτορας (ο) conductor *(on bus)* || **χωρίς εισπράκτορα** without conductor; one-man-operated *(exact fare required)*

εκδόσεις εισιτηρίων tickets

εκδοτήριο (το) tickets || **εκδοτήρια** ticket machines

εκεί there

έκθεση (η) exhibition

εκκλησία (η) church

έκπτωση (η) discount || **εκπτώσεις** sale

εκτελούνται έργα road works

εκτός except; unless || **εκτός λειτουργίας** out of order

έλα! come on!; come along!; come here!

ελαστικό (το) tyre || **σέρβις ελαστικών** tyre service

ελαττώνω to reduce || **ελαττώσατε ταχύτητα** reduce speed

έλεγχος (ο) control || **έλεγχος διαβατηρίων** passport control || **έλεγχος εισιτηρίων** check-in || **έλεγχος ελαστικών** tyre check || **έλεγχος επιβατών και αποσκευών** check-in || **αγορανομικός έλεγχος** approved prices || **υγειονομικός έλεγχος** approved by the health authorities

ελεύθερος/η/ο free; for hire

ελιά (η) olive; olive tree

έλκος (το) ulcer

Ελλάδα/Ελλάς (η) Greece

´Ελληνας/ίδα Greek *(man/woman)*

Ελληνικά (τα) Greek *(language)*

ελληνικός/ή/ό Greek *(thing)* || **Ελληνικά Ταχυδρομεία** Greek Post Office || **Ελληνική Δημοκρατία** Republic of Greece || **Ελληνική Λέσχη Αυτοκινήτου και Περιηγήσεων (ΕΛΠΑ)** The Automobile and Touring Club of Greece || **Ελληνικής κατασκευής** Made in Greece || **το Ελληνικό** Athens Airport || **Ελληνικός Οργανισμός Τουρισμού** Greek Tourist Organization || **Ελληνικό προϊόν** product of Greece

εμπρός forward; in front

εμφανίζω to develop *(film)* || **εμφάνιση παράδοση σε 1 ώρα** films developed in one hour

Α	α	A
Β	β	V
Γ	γ	G
Δ	δ	D
Ε	ε	E
Ζ	ζ	Z
Η	η	I
Θ	θ	Th
Ι	ι	I
Κ	κ	K
Λ	λ	L
Μ	μ	M
Ν	ν	N
Ξ	ξ	X
Ο	ο	O
Π	π	P
Ρ	ρ	R
Σ	σ,ς	S
Τ	τ	T
Υ	υ	I
Φ	φ	F
Χ	χ	H
Ψ	ψ	Ps
Ω	ω	O

εναντίον against
έναρξη (η) opening; beginning
ένας/μία/ένα one
ένδυμα (το) article of clothing || έτοιμα ενδύματα ready-to-wear
ένεση (η) injection
εννέα nine
ενοικιάζω to rent; to hire || ενοικιάζεται to let
ενοικιάσεις for hire
ενοίκιο (το) rent
εντάξει all right; OK
εντομοκτόνο (το) insecticide
έντυπο (το) form (to fill in)
έξη/ι six
έξοδος (η) exit; gate (at airport)
εξοχή (η) countryside
εξυπηρέτηση (η) service
έξω out; outside
εξωλέμβιες (οι) motorboats
εξώστης (ο) circle; balcony (in theatre)
εξωτερικός/ή/ό external || το εξωτερικό foreign countries (outside Greece) || εξωτερικού letters abroad (on post boxes) || πτήσεις εξωτερικού international flights
ΕΟΚ EEC
ΕΟΤ = Ελληνικός Οργανισμός Τουρισμού
επάγγελμα (το) occupation; profession
επείγον/επείγουσα urgent; express
επιβάτης/τρια passenger || διερχόμενοι επιβάτες passengers in transit
επιβατικά (τα) private cars
επιβεβαιώνω to confirm
επιβίβαση (η) boarding || κάρτα επιβιβάσεως boarding card
επιδόρπιο (το) dessert
επικίνδυνος/η/ο dangerous || επικίνδυνη κατωφέρεια dangerous incline

Α	α	A
Β	β	V
Γ	γ	G
Δ	δ	D
Ε	ε	E
Ζ	ζ	Z
Η	η	I
Θ	θ	Th
Ι	ι	I
Κ	κ	K
Λ	λ	L
Μ	μ	M
Ν	ν	N
Ξ	ξ	X
Ο	ο	O
Π	π	P
Ρ	ρ	R
Σ	σ,ς	S
Τ	τ	T
Υ	υ	I
Φ	φ	F
Χ	χ	H
Ψ	ψ	Ps
Ω	ω	O

επίσης also

επισκευή (η) repair ‖ **επισκευές** repairs

επίσκεψη (η) visit ‖ **ώρες επισκέψεων** visiting hours

επιστολή (η) letter ‖ **επιστολή επείγουσα** urgent or express letter ‖ **επιστολή συστημένη** registered letter

επιστροφή (η) return ‖ **επιστροφή νομισμάτων** returned coins ‖ **επιστροφές** returned goods

επιταγή (η) cheque ‖ **ταχυδρομική επιταγή** postal order

επόμενος/η/ο next

εποχή (η) season

επτά seven

Επτάνησα (τα) Ionian Islands

επώνυμο (το) surname

έργα (τα) road works

εργαλείο (το) tool

εργαστήριο (το) workshop

εργοστάσιο (το) factory

ερώτηση (η) question

εστιατόριο (το) restaurant

εσώρουχα (τα) underwear

εσωτερικός/ή/ό internal ‖ **εσωτερικού** letters – inland (on post boxes) ‖ **πτήσεις εσωτερικού** internal flights

εταιρ(ε)ία (η) company; firm

έτοιμος/η/ο ready

έτος (το) year

έτσι so; like this ‖ **έτσι κι έτσι** so-so

ευθεία (η) straight line ‖ **κατ' ευθείαν** straight on

ευθυγράμμιση (η) wheel alignment

ευκαιρία (η) opportunity; bargain

ευκολία (η) ease; convenience ‖ **ευκολίες πληρωμής** credit terms

Ευρώπη (η) Europe

ευχαριστώ thank you

εφημερίδα (η) newspaper

έχω to have

ζάλη (η) dizziness

Α	α	A
Β	β	V
Γ	γ	G
Δ	δ	D
Ε	ε	E
Ζ	ζ	Z
Η	η	I
Θ	θ	Th
Ι	ι	I
Κ	κ	K
Λ	λ	L
Μ	μ	M
Ν	ν	N
Ξ	ξ	X
Ο	ο	O
Π	π	P
Ρ	ρ	R
Σ	σ,ς	S
Τ	τ	T
Υ	υ	I
Φ	φ	F
Χ	χ	H
Ψ	ψ	Ps
Ω	ω	O

ζαμπόν (το) ham
ζάχαρη (η) sugar
ζαχαροπλαστείο (το) patisserie
ζέστη (η) heat || κάνει ζέστη it's hot
ζημιά (η) damage || πάσα ζημιά τιμωρείται anyone causing damage will be prosecuted
ζητώ to ask; to seek
ζήτω! hurray!
ζυγαριά (η) scales *(for weighing)*
ζυγοστάθμιση (η) wheel balancing
ζυμαρικά (τα) pastries
ζωγραφική (η) painting *(art)*
ζώνη (η) belt || ζώνη ασφαλείας safety belt
ζώο (το) animal
ζωολογικός κήπος zoo

η the *(with feminine nouns)*
ή or
HB UK
ηλεκτρισμός (ο) electricity
ηλεκτρονικός/ή/ό electronic || ηλεκτρονική ζυγοστάθμιση electronic wheel balancing || ηλεκτρονικός έλεγχος electronic check
ηλιακός/ή/ό solar
ηλίαση (η) sunstroke
ηλικία (η) age
ηλιοθεραπεία (η) sunbathing
ήλιος (ο) sun
'Ηλιος a dry white wine from Rhodes
ημέρα (η) day
ημερήσιος/α/ο daily
ημερομηνία (η) date || ημερομηνία αναχωρήσεως date of departure || ημερομηνία αφίξεως date of arrival || ημερομηνία γεννήσεως date of birth || ημερομηνία λήξεως expiry date
ημιδιατροφή (η) half board
Ηνωμένο Βασίλειο United Kingdom

A	α	A
B	β	V
Γ	γ	G
Δ	δ	D
E	ε	E
Z	ζ	Z
H	η	I
Θ	θ	Th
I	ι	I
K	κ	K
Λ	λ	L
M	μ	M
N	ν	N
Ξ	ξ	X
O	ο	O
Π	π	P
P	ρ	R
Σ	σ,ς	S
T	τ	T
Υ	υ	I
Φ	φ	F
X	χ	H
Ψ	ψ	Ps
Ω	ω	O

HΠA USA
ησυχία (η) calmness; quiet

θαλαμηπόλος (ο) room steward on boat
θάλασσα (η) sea || **θαλάσσιο αλεξίπτωτο** paragliding || **θαλάσσιο σκι** water-skiing || **θαλάσσια σπορ** watersports
θέατρο (το) theatre
θεός (ο) god
θεραπεία (η) treatment
θερινός/ή/ό summer || **θερινές διακοπές** summer holidays
θέρμανση (η) heating
θερμίδα (η) calorie
θερμοστάτης (ο) thermostat
θέση (η) place; seat || **θέση στάθμευσης αυτοκινήτων** parking || **διακεκριμένη θέση** business class || **κράτηση θέσης** seat reservation || **οικονομική θέση** economy class || **πρώτη θέση** first class
Θεσσαλονίκη (η) Salonica
Θίσβη a white wine from Cyprus
θύελλα (η) storm
θύρα (η) door; gate (at airport) || **πυροστεγής θύρα** fire door
θυρίδα (η), θυρίς (η) ticket window || **θυρίς καταθέσεων** deposits; night safe (bank)
θυροτηλέφωνο (το) emergency phone (on train)
θυρωρείο (το) porter

Ιανουάριος (ο) January
ιατρική περίθαλψη medical treatment
ιατρός (ο/η) doctor
ιδιοκτήτης/τρια owner
ιδιωτικός/ή/ό private || **ιδιωτικός χώρος** private; keep off/out; no parking
ιθαγένεια (η) nationality
ιματιοθήκη (η) cloakroom
Ιόνιο Πέλαγο Ionian sea
Ιόνιοι Νήσοι Ionian Islands

Α	α	A
Β	β	V
Γ	γ	G
Δ	δ	D
Ε	ε	E
Ζ	ζ	Z
Η	η	I
Θ	θ	Th
Ι	ι	I
Κ	κ	K
Λ	λ	L
Μ	μ	M
Ν	ν	N
Ξ	ξ	X
Ο	ο	O
Π	π	P
Ρ	ρ	R
Σ	σ,ς	S
Τ	τ	T
Υ	υ	I
Φ	φ	F
Χ	χ	H
Ψ	ψ	Ps
Ω	ω	O

Ιούλιος (o) July
Ιούνιος (o) June
ιππασία (η) riding
ιπποδρομίες (οι) horse racing
ιππόδρομος (o) racetrack
ιππόκαμπος (o) jet-skiing
ιπτάμενος/η/ο flying || ιπτάμενο δελφίνι hydrofoil
Ισθμός (o) canal || ο Ισθμός της Κορίνθου the Corinth canal
ισόγειο (το) ground floor
Ισπανία (η) Spain
ισπανικός/ή/ό Spanish (thing)
Ισπανός/ίδα Spaniard (man/woman)
ιστιοπλοΐα (η) sailing
Ιταλία (η) Italy
ιταλικός/ή/ό Italian (thing)
Ιταλός/ίδα Italian (man/woman)
ΙΧ private cars (parking sign)
ιχθυοπωλείο (το) fishmonger's

κάβα (η) trolley/rack for drinks || κάβα οινοπνευματωδών spirits trolley
κάβουρας (o) crab
καζίνο (το) casino
καθαριστήριο (το) dry-cleaner's
καθαρίστρια (η) cleaner
καθαρός/ή/ό clean || Καθαρά Δευτέρα Ash Wednesday
κάθε every; each
καθεδρικός ναός cathedral
καθημερινά daily || καθημερινά δρομολόγια daily departures
κάθισμα (το) seat
καθολικός/ή/ό Catholic
καθυστέρηση (η) delay
και and
καιρός (o) weather
κακάο (το) drinking chocolate

Α	α	A
Β	β	V
Γ	γ	G
Δ	δ	D
Ε	ε	E
Ζ	ζ	Z
Η	η	I
Θ	θ	Th
Ι	ι	I
Κ	κ	K
Λ	λ	L
Μ	μ	M
Ν	ν	N
Ξ	ξ	X
Ο	ο	O
Π	π	P
Ρ	ρ	R
Σ	σ,ς	S
Τ	τ	T
Υ	υ	I
Φ	φ	F
Χ	χ	H
Ψ	ψ	Ps
Ω	ω	O

κακοκαιρία (η) bad weather
καλά well; all right
καλάθι (το) basket
καλαμάρι (το) squid
καλημέρα good morning
καληνύχτα good night
καλησπέρα good evening
καλλιστεία (τα) beauty contest
καλοκαίρι (το) summer
καλλυντικά (τα) cosmetics
καλοριφέρ (το) central heating; radiator
καλοψημένο well done *(meat)*
καλσόν (το) tights
κάλτσα (η) sock; stocking
καμαριέρα (η) chambermaid
καμπή (η) bend *(in road)*
καμπίνα (η) cabin
κανάλι (το) canal; channel *(TV)*
κανάτα (η) jug
κανέλα (η) cinnamon
κανό (το) canoe
κάνω to do
καπαρτίνα (η) raincoat
καπέλο (το) hat
καπετάνιος (ο) captain *(of ship)*
καπνίζω to smoke; **μην καπνίζετε** no smoking
κάπνισμα (το) smoking ‖ **απαγορεύεται το κάπνισμα** no smoking
καπνιστής (ο) smoker ‖ **είδη καπνιστού** tobacconist's
καπνοπωλείο (το) tobacconist
καπνός (ο) smoke; tobacco
κάποτε sometimes
καράβι (το) boat; ship
καραμέλα (η) sweet(s)
κάρβουνο (το) coal ‖ **στα κάρβουνα** charcoal-grilled
καρδιά (η) heart

Α	α	A
Β	β	V
Γ	γ	G
Δ	δ	D
Ε	ε	E
Ζ	ζ	Z
Η	η	I
Θ	θ	Th
Ι	ι	I
Κ	κ	K
Λ	λ	L
Μ	μ	M
Ν	ν	N
Ξ	ξ	X
Ο	ο	O
Π	π	P
Ρ	ρ	R
Σ	σ,ς	S
Τ	τ	T
Υ	υ	I
Φ	φ	F
Χ	χ	H
Ψ	ψ	Ps
Ω	ω	O

καρμπιρατέρ (το) carburettor

καρναβάλι (το) carnival

καροτσάκι (το) pushchair

καρπούζι (το) watermelon

κάρτα (η) card || **κάρτα απεριόριστων διαδρομών** rail card for unlimited travel || **κάρτα επιβιβάσεως** boarding card || **καρτ-ποστάλ** postcard || **επαγγελματική κάρτα** business card || **μόνο με κάρτα** cardholders only || **πιστωτικές κάρτες** credit cards

καρύδα (η) coconut

καρύδι (το) walnut

καρχαρίας (ο) shark

κασέτα (η) tape *(for recording)*

κασετόφωνο (το) tape recorder

κάστανο (το) chestnut

Καστέλλι Μίνος a medium-dry red wine from Cyprus

κάστρο (το) castle; fortress

κατάθεση (η) deposit; statement to police || **καταθέσεις υπό προειδοποίηση** deposit accounts only *(in banks)*

καταιγίδα (η) storm

καταλαβαίνω to understand || **καταλαβαίνεις;** do you understand? *(familiar form)* || **καταλαβαίνετε;** do you understand? *(polite form)*

κατάλογος (ο) list; menu; directory || **τηλεφωνικός κατάλογος** telephone directory

καταπραϋντικό (το) tranquillizer

κατασκευή (η): **Ελληνικής κατασκευής** Made in Greece

κατασκήνωση (η) camping

κατάστημα (το) shop

κατάστρωμα (το) deck

κατέϊφι (το) a sweet made of shredded pastry stuffed with almonds

κατεπείγον/κατεπείγουσα urgent; express

κατεψυγμένος/η/ο frozen

κατηγορία (η) class *(of hotel)*; accusation

κατηγορώ to accuse

κατσαρόλα (η) saucepan

Α	α	A
Β	β	V
Γ	γ	G
Δ	δ	D
Ε	ε	E
Ζ	ζ	Z
Η	η	I
Θ	θ	Th
Ι	ι	I
Κ	κ	K
Λ	λ	L
Μ	μ	M
Ν	ν	N
Ξ	ξ	X
Ο	ο	O
Π	π	P
Ρ	ρ	R
Σ	σ,ς	S
Τ	τ	T
Υ	υ	I
Φ	φ	F
Χ	χ	H
Ψ	ψ	Ps
Ω	ω	O

κατσίκα (η) goat
κατσικάκι (το) kid *(young goat)*
κάτω under; lower
καύσιμα (τα) fuel
καφέ brown
καφενείο (το) coffee house
καφές (ο) coffee *(usually Turkish coffee)* || **καφές βαρύς γλυκύς** very sweet coffee || **καφές γλυκύς** sweet coffee || **καφές μέτριος** medium sweet coffee || **καφές σκέτος** coffee without sugar || **καφές στιγμιαίος** instant coffee || **καφές φραπέ** iced coffee
καφετηρία (η) cafeteria
κέικ (το) cake
κ.εκ cubic capacity
κεντρικός/ή/ό central || **κεντρική βιβλιοθήκη** central library
κέντρο (το) centre; café || **κέντρο αλλοδαπών** immigration office || **κέντρο διασκεδάσεως** nightclub || **κέντρο εισιτηρίων** ticket office || **κέντρο πληροφόρησης νεότητος** youth information centre || **αθλητικό κέντρο** sports centre || **εξοχικό κέντρο** country café || **τηλεφωνικό κέντρο** telephone exchange
κεράσι (το) cherry
Κέρκυρα (η) Corfu
κέρμα (το) coin
κερνώ to buy a drink
κεφαλή (η) head
κέφι (το) good humour
κεφτές (ο) meatball
κήπος (ο) garden || **δημόσιος κήπος** public garden || **είδη κήπου** garden centre || **ζωολογικός κήπος** zoo
κιβώτιο (το) box || **κιβώτιο ταχύτητων** gearbox
κιλό (το) kilo
κιμάς (ο) minced meat
κίνδυνος (ο) danger || **κίνδυνος θάνατος** extreme danger || **κίνδυνος πυρκαγιάς στο δάσος** fire risk *(in forest)* || **κώδων κινδύνου** emergency signal
κινηματογράφος (ο) cinema

Α	α	A
Β	β	V
Γ	γ	G
Δ	δ	D
Ε	ε	E
Ζ	ζ	Z
Η	η	I
Θ	θ	Th
Ι	ι	I
Κ	κ	K
Λ	λ	L
Μ	μ	M
Ν	ν	N
Ξ	ξ	X
Ο	ο	O
Π	π	P
Ρ	ρ	R
Σ	σ,ς	S
Τ	τ	T
Υ	υ	I
Φ	φ	F
Χ	χ	H
Ψ	ψ	Ps
Ω	ω	O

κινητήρας (ο) engine
Κιτρό a slightly sour white wine from Naxos
κλάξόν (το) horn *(in car)*
κλειδί (το) spanner; key
κλειστός/ή/ό closed
κλήση (η) summons
κλίμα (το) climate
κλινική (η) clinic
κοινωνικός/ή/ό social || **κοινωνικές ασφαλίσεις**
  national insurance
Κοκκινέλι a sweet red wine
κόκκινος/η/ο red
κοκορέτσι (το) stuffed lamb entrails roasted on a spit
κολοκυθάκι (το) courgette
κολοκίθι (το) marrow
κόλπος gulf
κολύμπι (το) swimming
κολώνα (η) pillar
κομμωτήριο (το) hairdresser's
κομμωτής/τρια hairstylist
κομπολόι (το) string of beads
κομπόστα (η) stewed fruit
κονιάκ (το) brandy
κονσέρβα (η) tinned fruit
κονσέρτο (το) concert
κοντά near
κόρη (η) daughter
κορίτσι (το) young girl
κόσμημα (το) jewellery || **κοσμήματα** jeweller's
κοστούμι man's suit
κότα (η) hen
κοτολέτα (η) chop
κοτόπουλο (το) chicken
κουζίνα (η) kitchen
Κουμανταρία a very sweet dessert wine from Cyprus
κουνέλι (το) rabbit

A	α	A
B	β	V
Γ	γ	G
Δ	δ	D
E	ε	E
Z	ζ	Z
H	η	I
Θ	θ	Th
I	ι	I
K	κ	K
Λ	λ	L
M	μ	M
N	ν	N
Ξ	ξ	X
O	ο	O
Π	π	P
P	ρ	R
Σ	σ,ς	S
T	τ	T
Υ	υ	I
Φ	φ	F
X	χ	H
Ψ	ψ	Ps
Ω	ω	O

κουνούπι (το) mosquito
κουνουπίδι (το) cauliflower
κουπί (το) oar
κουρείο (το) barber's shop
κουταλάκι (το) teaspoon
κουτάλι (το) spoon
κουτί (το) box
κραγιόν (το) lipstick
κρασί (το) wine || **κρασί γλυκό** sweet wine || **κρασί ερυθρό** red wine || **κρασί λευκό** white wine || **κρασί μαύρο** red wine || **κρασί ξηρό** dry wine || **κρασί ροζέ** rosé wine
κρατήσεις (οι) bookings; reservations || **κρατήσεις ξενοδοχείων** hotel bookings
κράτηση (η): **κράτηση θέσης** seat reservation || **υπό κράτηση** in custody
κρέας (το) meat || **κρέας αρνίσιο** lamb || **κρέας βοδινό** beef || **κρέας χοιρινό** pork
κρεββάτι (το) bed
κρεββατοκάμαρα (η) bedroom
κρέμα (η) cream || **κρέμα σαντιγύ** real cream
κρεμμύδι (το) onion
κρεοπωλείο (το) butcher's shop
κρεοπώλης (ο) butcher
Κρήτη (η) Crete
κρουαζιέρα (η) cruise
κρουασάν (το) croissant
κρύος/α/ο cold || **κάνει κρύο** it's cold
κτηνιατρείο (το) veterinary surgery
κυβερνήτης (ο) captain (of aircraft)
κυβικά εκατοστά cubic capacity
Κυκλάδες (οι) Cyclades
κυκλοφορία (η) traffic; circulation || **κυκλοφορία εξ αντιθέτου κατευθύνσεως** oncoming traffic || **κυκλοφορία επί μίας λωρίδος** merge (traffic)
κυλικείο (το) cafeteria
κυλιόμενες κλίμακες/σκάλες escalators

Α	α	A
Β	β	V
Γ	γ	G
Δ	δ	D
Ε	ε	E
Ζ	ζ	Z
Η	η	I
Θ	θ	Th
Ι	ι	I
Κ	κ	K
Λ	λ	L
Μ	μ	M
Ν	ν	N
Ξ	ξ	X
Ο	ο	O
Π	π	P
Ρ	ρ	R
Σ	σ,ς	S
Τ	τ	T
Υ	υ	I
Φ	φ	F
Χ	χ	H
Ψ	ψ	Ps
Ω	ω	O

Κύπρος (η) Cyprus
Κύπριος/Κυπρία from Cyprus; Cypriot (man/woman)
κυρία (η) Mrs; lady
Κυριακή (η) Sunday
κύριος (ο) Mr; gentleman
κώδικας (ο) code ‖ κώδικας οδικής κυκλοφορίας
highway code ‖ ταχυδρομικός κώδικας postcode ‖
τηλεφωνικός κώδικας dialling code
κώδων (ο) bell

λάδι (το) oil
λαϊκός/ή/ό of the people; popular ‖ λαϊκή μουσική
popular music ‖ λαϊκή τέχνη folk art
λάστιχο (το) tyre; rubber; elastic
λαχανικά (τα) vegetables
λαχείο (το) lottery ‖ κρατικό λαχείο state lottery
λεμονάδα (η) lemon squash
λεμόνι (το) lemon ‖ χυμός λεμονιού lemon juice
λεξικό (το) dictionary
λεπτό (το) minute
λέσχη (η) club ‖ Ελληνική Λέσχη Αυτοκινήτου και
Περιηγήσεων Automobile and Touring Club of Greece
λευκός/ή/ό white ‖ λευκά είδη household linen
λεφτά (τα) money
λεωφορείο (το) bus
λεωφόρος (η) avenue
λήξη (η) expiry
λιανικός/ή/ό retail ‖ λιανική πώληση retail sale
λίγος/η/ο a few; a little ‖ λίγο ψημένο rare (meat)
λιθρίνι (το) grey mullet
λικέρ (το) liqueur
λιμάνι (το) port; harbour
Λιμενικό Σώμα coastguard ‖ Άμεση Επέμβαση
coastguard
λιμήν (ο) port
λίπανση (η) lubrication service
λίρα (η) pound ‖ Αγγλική λίρα pound sterling

Α	α	A
Β	β	V
Γ	γ	G
Δ	δ	D
Ε	ε	E
Ζ	ζ	Z
Η	η	I
Θ	θ	Th
Ι	ι	I
Κ	κ	K
Λ	λ	L
Μ	μ	M
Ν	ν	N
Ξ	ξ	X
Ο	ο	O
Π	π	P
Ρ	ρ	R
Σ	σ,ς	S
Τ	τ	T
Υ	υ	I
Φ	φ	F
Χ	χ	H
Ψ	ψ	Ps
Ω	ω	O

λίτρο (το) litre
λογαριασμός (ο) bill ‖ διπλότυπος λογαριασμός duplicate bill
λουκάνικο (το) sausage
λουκανόπιτα (η) sausage pie
λουκούμι (το) Turkish delight
λουτρό (το) bathroom; bath
λύσσα (η) rabies

μαγαζί (το) shop
μαγειρεύω to cook
μαγιό (το) swimsuit
Μάιος (ο) May
μαϊντανός (ο) parsley
μακαρόνια (τα) macaroni ‖ μακαρόνια παστίτσιο macaroni with minced meat and white sauce
Μαλβοίσια a red wine from Sparta
μάλιστα yes
μαλλί (το) wool
μαλλιά (τα) hair
μάλλινος/η/ο woollen
μαμά (η) mum
μανιτάρι (το) mushroom
μανταρίνι (το) tangerine
μαντήλι (το) handkerchief
Μαντηρίας a medium-dry white wine
Μάντικο a dry red wine from Crete
μαξιλάρι (το) pillow; cushion
μαργαρίνη (η) margarine
μαργαριτάρι (το) pearl
μάρμαρο (το) marble
μαρμελάδα (η) marmalade
μαρούλι (το) lettuce
Μάρτιος (ο) March
Μαυροδάφνη a sweet red dessert wine
μαύρος/η/ο black
μαχαίρι (το) knife

Α	α	A
Β	β	V
Γ	γ	G
Δ	δ	D
Ε	ε	E
Ζ	ζ	Z
Η	η	I
Θ	θ	Th
Ι	ι	I
Κ	κ	K
Λ	λ	L
Μ	μ	M
Ν	ν	N
Ξ	ξ	X
Ο	ο	O
Π	π	P
Ρ	ρ	R
Σ	σ,ς	S
Τ	τ	T
Υ	υ	I
Φ	φ	F
Χ	χ	H
Ψ	ψ	Ps
Ω	ω	O

μαχαιροπήρουνα (τα) cutlery
με with
μεγάλος/η/ο large; big
μέγαρο (το) palace; large building containing apartments
μέγεθος (το) size
μεζεδάκια (τα) selection of appetizers and salads served as a starter
μέλι (το) honey
μελιτζάνα (η) aubergine
μέλος (το) member || τα μέλη του πληρώματος crew members
μενού (το) menu
μέρα (η) day
μερίδα (η) portion
μέσα in; inside
μεσάνυκτα (τα) midnight
μεσημέρι (το) midday
Μεσόγειος (η) Mediterranean Sea
μέσω via
μετά after
μετάξι (το) silk
μεταξύ between; among || εν τω μεταξύ meanwhile
μεταφράζω to translate
μεταχειρισμένος/η/ο used; second-hand || μεταχειρισμένα αυτοκίνητα second-hand cars
μετεωρολογικός σταθμός weather centre
μετρητά (τα) cash
μετρό (το) underground (railway)
μη do not || μη καπνίζετε no smoking || μη κόπτετε άνθη do not pick flowers || μη πατάτε το πράσινο keep off the grass || μη ρίπτετε σκουπίδια no dumping (of rubbish) || μη σταθμεύετε no parking || μη στηρίζεστε στην πόρτα do not lean against the door
μηδέν zero
μήλο (το) apple
μηλόπιτα (η) apple pie

Α	α	A
Β	β	V
Γ	γ	G
Δ	δ	D
Ε	ε	E
Ζ	ζ	Z
Η	η	I
Θ	θ	Th
Ι	ι	I
Κ	κ	K
Λ	λ	L
Μ	μ	M
Ν	ν	N
Ξ	ξ	X
Ο	ο	O
Π	π	P
Ρ	ρ	R
Σ	σ,ς	S
Τ	τ	T
Υ	υ	I
Φ	φ	F
Χ	χ	H
Ψ	ψ	Ps
Ω	ω	O

μήνας (ο) month || μήνας του μέλιτος honeymoon
μητέρα (η) mother
μηχανή (η) machine; engine || φορητή μηχανή portable camera
μηχανικός (ο) mechanic; engineer
μια a/an; one *(with feminine nouns)*
μίζα (η) starter *(in car)*
μικρός/ή/ό small
μόδα (η) fashion || ανδρική μόδα fashions for men
μολύβι (το) pencil
μόλυνση (η) infection
μοναστήρι (το) monastery
μονόδρομος (ο) one-way street
μονοπάτι (το) path
μόνος/η/ο alone; only || μόνο είσοδος/έξοδος entrance/exit only
μονός/ή/ό single
Μόντε Χρήστος a sweet red wine from Cyprus
μοσχάρι (το) calf; veal || μοσχάρι κρασάτο veal cooked in wine || μοσχάρι ψητό roast veal
Μοσχάτο a dark red dessert wine with a muscatel flavour
μοτοσυκλέτα (η) motorcycle
μουσείο (το) museum || Αρχαιολογικό Μουσείο Archaeological Museum || Μουσείο Λαϊκής Τέχνης Folk Museum
μουσική (η) music || μουσικά όργανα musical instruments
μουστάρδα (η) mustard
μπακάλης (ο) grocer
μπακλαβάς (ο) a sweet made of flaky pastry stuffed with almonds and syrup
μπαμπάς (ο) dad
μπανάνα (η) banana
μπάνιο (το) bathroom; bath
μπαρμπούνι (το) red mullet
μπαταρία (η) battery

Α	α	A
Β	β	V
Γ	γ	G
Δ	δ	D
Ε	ε	E
Ζ	ζ	Z
Η	η	I
Θ	θ	Th
Ι	ι	I
Κ	κ	K
Λ	λ	L
Μ	μ	M
Ν	ν	N
Ξ	ξ	X
Ο	ο	O
Π	π	P
Ρ	ρ	R
Σ	σ,ς	S
Τ	τ	T
Υ	υ	I
Φ	φ	F
Χ	χ	H
Ψ	ψ	Ps
Ω	ω	O

μπαχαρικά (τα) spices
μπέικον (το) bacon
μπιζέλι (το) pea
μπισκότο (το) biscuit
μπιφτέκι (το) steak
μπλούζα (η) blouse
μπουζούκι (το) bouzouki *(musical instrument)*
μπουκάλα (η) bottle || **μπουκάλα μεγάλη** large bottle || **μικρή μπουκάλα** half-bottle
μπουρνούζι (το) bathrobe
μπράβο! bravo!
μπριζόλα (η) chop
μπύρα (η) beer
Μυκήναι/ες (οι) Mycenae
μύτη (η) nose
μωρό (το) baby || **για μωρά** for babies
μωσαϊκό (το) mosaic

ναι yes
ναός (ο) temple; church || **καθεδρικός ναός** cathedral
ναύλο (το) fare
νάυλον nylon
ναυλωμένος/η/ο chartered || **ναυλωμένη πτήση** charter flight
ναυτία (η) travel sickness
ναυτικός όμιλος sailing club
ναυτιλιακά yacht chandler
νεκροταφείο (το) cemetery
Νεοελληνικά (τα) Modern Greek
νερό (το) water || **επιτραπέζιο νερό** still mineral water || **μεταλλικό νερό** sparkling mineral water || **πόσιμο νερό** drinking water
νεφρός (ο) kidney
νεωτερισμός (ο) improvement; novelty || **κατάστημα νεωτερισμού** novelties; fashions
νηπιαγωγείο (το) nursery school
νησί (το) island

Α	α	A
Β	β	V
Γ	γ	G
Δ	δ	D
Ε	ε	E
Ζ	ζ	Z
Η	η	I
Θ	θ	Th
Ι	ι	I
Κ	κ	K
Λ	λ	L
Μ	μ	M
Ν	ν	N
Ξ	ξ	X
Ο	ο	O
Π	π	P
Ρ	ρ	R
Σ	σ,ς	S
Τ	τ	T
Υ	υ	I
Φ	φ	F
Χ	χ	H
Ψ	ψ	Ps
Ω	ω	O

νησίδα (η) traffic island; central reservation

νίκη (η) victory

Νοέμβριος (ο) November

νοίκι (το) rent

νομαρχία (η) administration offices of a *nomos*

νόμισμα (το) coin || επιστροφή νομισμάτων returned coins

νομισματοδέχτης (ο) coin-operated telephone || αστικός νομισματοδέχτης coin-operated phone for local calls || υπεραστικός νομισματοδέχτης coin-operated phone for trunk calls

νομός (ο) *nomos*, Greek administrative unit

νοσοκομείο (το) hospital

νοσοκόμος/α nurse

νότος (ο) south

ντολμαδάκια (τα) stuffed vine leaves

ντομάτα (η) tomato

ντουζίνα (η) dozen

ντους (το) shower *(in bath)*

νύκτα (η) night

νυκτερινός/ή/ό all-night *(chemist's, etc)*

νύχτα (η) night

νυχτικό (το) nightdress

ξεναγός (ο/η) guide

ξενοδοχείο (το) hotel || κρατήσεις ξενοδοχείων hotel reservations

ξένος/η/ο strange; foreign || ξένος/η stranger; foreigner; visitor

ξενώνας (ο) guesthouse

ξεπούλημα (το) sale

ξηρός/ή/ό dry || ξηροί καρποί dried fruit and nuts

ξιφίας (ο) swordfish

ξύδι (το) vinegar

ξυριστική μηχανή (η) safety razor

οδηγία (η) instruction || οδηγίες χρήσεως instructions for use

Α	α	A
Β	β	V
Γ	γ	G
Δ	δ	D
Ε	ε	E
Ζ	ζ	Z
Η	η	I
Θ	θ	Th
Ι	ι	I
Κ	κ	K
Λ	λ	L
Μ	μ	M
Ν	ν	N
Ξ	ξ	X
Ο	ο	O
Π	π	P
Ρ	ρ	R
Σ	σ,ς	S
Τ	τ	T
Υ	υ	I
Φ	φ	F
Χ	χ	H
Ψ	ψ	Ps
Ω	ω	O

οδηγός (ο) driver; guidebook || **σήμα στον οδηγό** signal to the driver *('stop' button in bus)*

οδηγώ to drive

οδική βοήθεια breakdown service

οδοντιατρείο (το) dental surgery

οδοντίατρος/οδοντογιατρός (ο/η) dentist

οδοντόπαστα (η) toothpaste

οδοντοστοιχία (η) denture(s)

οδός (η) road; street

Οθέλλος a medium-dry red wine from Cyprus

οικογένεια (η) family

οικονομική θέση economy class

οίκος (ο) house || **οίκος μόδας** fashion house || **οπτικός οίκος** optician

οινομαγειρείον (το) licensed restaurant

οινοπνευματώδη ποτά spirits

οίνος (ο) wine

οκταπόδι (το) octopus

οκτώ eight

Οκτώβριος (ο) October

ολισθυρόν οδόστρωμα slippery road surface

όλος/η/ο all of

Ολυμπία (η) Olympia

Ολυμπιακή (η)/**Ολυμπιακές Αερογραμμές** Olympic Airways

Ολυμπιακό Στάδιο Olympic stadium

Ολυμπιακοί Αγώνες Olympic games

Όλυμπος (ο) Mount Olympus

ομελέτα (η) omelette

όμιλος (ο) club || **ναυτικός όμιλος** sailing club

ομπρέλλα (η) umbrella

όνομα (το) name

ονοματεπώνυμο (το) full name

όπερα (η) opera

οπτικός οίκος optician

οργανισμός (ο) organization || **Οργανισμός**

Α	α	A
Β	β	V
Γ	γ	G
Δ	δ	D
Ε	ε	E
Ζ	ζ	Z
Η	η	I
Θ	θ	Th
Ι	ι	I
Κ	κ	K
Λ	λ	L
Μ	μ	M
Ν	ν	N
Ξ	ξ	X
Ο	ο	O
Π	π	P
Ρ	ρ	R
Σ	σ,ς	S
Τ	τ	T
Υ	υ	I
Φ	φ	F
Χ	χ	H
Ψ	ψ	Ps
Ω	ω	O

Σιδηροδρόμων Ελλάδος Greek Railways || Οργανισμός Τηλεπικοινωνιών Ελλάδος Greek Telecommunications

οργανωμένος/η/ο organized || οργανωμένα ταξίδια organized tours

ορεκτικό (το) starter

όρεξη (η) appetite || καλή όρεξη enjoy your meal!

ορθόδοξος/η/ο orthodox

όρος (ο) condition || όροι ενοικιάσεως conditions of hire

όρος (το) mountain

όροφος (ο) floor; storey

ΟΤΕ = Οργανισμός Τηλεπικοινωνιών Ελλάδος

Ουαλία (η) Wales

ουδέν: ουδέν προς δήλωση nothing to declare

ούζο (το) ouzo *(aniseed-flavoured spirit)*

ουρά (η) tail; queue

οχταπόδι (το) octopus

όχι no

παγάκι (το) ice cube

παγιδάκι (το) lamb chop

πάγος (ο) ice

παγωμένος/η/ο frozen || μία μπύρα παγωμένη one cold beer

παγωτό (το) ice cream

παιδικός/ή/ό for children || παιδικά children's wear || παιδικός σταθμός crèche || παιδικά σωσίβια children's life jackets

πακέτο (το) parcel; packet

Παλλήνη a white wine from Attica

παλτό (το) coat

πάνα (η) nappy

Παναγία (η) the Virgin Mary

πανεπιστήμιο (το) university

Πανσιόν guesthouse

πάντοτε always

παντελόνι (το) trousers

παντοπωλείο (το) grocer's

Α	α	A
Β	β	V
Γ	γ	G
Δ	δ	D
Ε	ε	E
Ζ	ζ	Z
Η	η	I
Θ	θ	Th
Ι	ι	I
Κ	κ	K
Λ	λ	L
Μ	μ	M
Ν	ν	N
Ξ	ξ	X
Ο	ο	O
Π	π	P
Ρ	ρ	R
Σ	σ,ς	S
Τ	τ	T
Υ	υ	I
Φ	φ	F
Χ	χ	H
Ψ	ψ	Ps
Ω	ω	O

παπάς (o) priest
Πάπας (o) Pope
πάπλωμα (το) duvet
παππούς (o) grandfather
παπούτσι (το) shoe
παραγγελία (η) order; message
παραγωγή (η) production || Ελληνικής παραγωγής produce of Greece
παράθυρο (το) window
παρακαλώ please
παρακαμπτήριος diversion
παραλία (η) seashore
Παρασκευή (η) Friday
παράσταση (η) performance
Παρθενών/ώνας (o) the Parthenon
πάρκο (το) park
παρμπρίζ (το) windscreen
πάστα (η) pastry
παστέλι (το) honey and sesame seed bar
Πάσχα (το) Easter
πατάτα (η) potato || πατάτες πουρέ creamed potatoes || πατάτες τηγανιτές chips || πατάτες φούρνου roast potatoes
πατέρας (o) father
πατώ to step || μη πατάτε το πράσινο keep off the grass
παυσίπονο (το) painkiller
πέδιλα (τα) sandals
πεζοδρόμιο (το) pavement
πεζόδρομος (o) pedestrian area
πεζός (o) pedestrian
Πειραιάς/Πειραιεύς Piraeus
πελάτης/τρια customer
Πελοπόννησος (η) Peloponnese
Πέμπτη (η) Thursday
πένα (η) pen
πέντε five
Πεντέλη a medium-dry red wine

A	α	A
B	β	V
Γ	γ	G
Δ	δ	D
E	ε	E
Z	ζ	Z
H	η	I
Θ	θ	Th
I	ι	I
K	κ	K
Λ	λ	L
M	μ	M
N	ν	N
Ξ	ξ	X
O	o	O
Π	π	P
P	ρ	R
Σ	σ,ς	S
T	τ	T
Υ	υ	I
Φ	φ	F
X	χ	H
Ψ	ψ	Ps
Ω	ω	O

πεπόνι (το) melon
περιοδικό (το) magazine
περιοχή (η) area
περίπατος (ο) walk
περίπτερο (το) kiosk
περιστέρι (το) pigeon; dove
πετονιά (η) fishing/butterfly net
πετρέλαιο (το) oil; diesel fuel
πετσέτα (η) napkin; towel
πεύκο (το) pine tree
πηγαίνω to go
πιάτο (το) plate
πιέσατε push
πίεση (η) pressure
πιζάμες (οι) pyjamas
πιλάφι (το) pilau *(rice dish)*
πιλότος (ο) pilot
πινακίδα (η) sign; name/number plate ‖ προστατεύετε
  τας πινακίδας do not deface signs
πινακοθήκη (η) art gallery
πίπα (η) pipe
πιπέρι (το) pepper ‖ πιπεριές γεμιστές stuffed peppers
πισίνα (η) swimming pool
πιστοποιητικό (το) certificate ‖ πιστοποιητικό
  εμβολιασμού vaccination certificate
πιστωτικές κάρτες credit cards
πίσω behind; back
πίτα (η) pie
πίτζα (η) pizza
πιτζαρία (η) pizzeria
πλαζ (η) beach
πλάι next to
πλατεία (η) square
πλατίνες (οι) points *(in car)*
πλεκτά (τα) knitwear
πληροφορίες (οι) information ‖ πληροφορίες
  δρομολογίων travel information

Α	α	A
Β	β	V
Γ	γ	G
Δ	δ	D
Ε	ε	E
Ζ	ζ	Z
Η	η	I
Θ	θ	Th
Ι	ι	I
Κ	κ	K
Λ	λ	L
Μ	μ	M
Ν	ν	N
Ξ	ξ	X
Ο	ο	O
Π	π	P
Ρ	ρ	R
Σ	σ,ς	S
Τ	τ	T
Υ	υ	I
Φ	φ	F
Χ	χ	H
Ψ	ψ	Ps
Ω	ω	O

πλήρωμα (το) crew || **τα μέλη του πληρώματος** members of the crew

πληρωμή (η) payment || **ευκολίες πληρωμής** credit facilities || **προς πληρωμή** insert money

πληρώνω to pay

πλοίο (το) ship

πλυντήριο (το) washing machine || **πλυντήριο αυτοκινήτων** car wash

πλύσιμο wash(ing) || **πλύσιμο αυτοκινήτων** car wash

ποδήλατο (το) bicycle || **ποδήλατο της θάλασσας** pedalo

ποδηλάται (οι) cyclists

πόδι (το) foot; leg

ποδόσφαιρο (το) football

πόλη/ις (η) town

πολυκατάστημα (το) department store

πολυκατοικία (η) block of flats

πολυκλινική (η) privately-run general clinic

πολύς/πολλή/πολύ many; much

πονόδοντος (ο) toothache

πονοκέφαλος (ο) headache

πονόλαιμος (ο) sore throat

πόνος (ο) pain

πόρτα (η) door

πορτοκαλάδα (η) orange squash

πορτοκάλι (το) orange || **χυμός πορτοκάλι** orange juice

πορτοφόλι (το) wallet

πόσα; how many?

πόσο; how much ? || **πόσο κάνει;** how much is it ?

ποσοστό (το) rate; percentage || **ποσοστό υπηρεσίας** service charge || **συμπεριλαμβανομένου ποσοστού υπηρεσίας** including service charge

ποσότητα (η) quantity

πότε; when?

ποτέ never

ποτήρι (το) glass *(for drinking)*

ποτό (το) drink

Α	α	A
Β	β	V
Γ	γ	G
Δ	δ	D
Ε	ε	E
Ζ	ζ	Z
Η	η	I
Θ	θ	Th
Ι	ι	I
Κ	κ	K
Λ	λ	L
Μ	μ	M
Ν	ν	N
Ξ	ξ	X
Ο	ο	O
Π	π	P
Ρ	ρ	R
Σ	σ,ς	S
Τ	τ	T
Υ	υ	I
Φ	φ	F
Χ	χ	H
Ψ	ψ	Ps
Ω	ω	O

πού; where ? ‖ πού είναι; where is it ?
πουκάμισο (το) shirt
πούλμαν (το) coach
πουρμπουάρ (το) tip *(to waiter, etc)*
πούρο (το) cigar
πράκτορας (ο) agent
πρακτορείο (το) agency
πράσινος/η/ο green
πρατήριο (το) specialist shop ‖ πρατήριο βενζίνης petrol station ‖ πρατήριο άρτου baker's
πρεσβεία (η) embassy
πρεσβευτής (ο) ambassador
πρίζα (η) plug; socket
πριν before
πρόγευμα (το) breakfast
πρόγραμμα (το) programme
πρόεδρος (ο) president ‖ προεδρικό μέγαρο presidential palace
προειδοποίηση (η) warning
προέλευση (η) point of embarkation
προϊόν (το) product ‖ Ελληνικό προϊόν product of Greece
προκαταβολή (η) deposit
προκρατήσεις (οι) advance bookings
προξενείο (το) consulate
πρόξενος (ο) consul
προορισμός (ο) destination
προπληρώνω to pay in advance
Προ-πο Greek football pools
προσγείωση (η) landing
προσδεθείτε fasten your safety belts
πρόσκληση (η) invitation
προσοχή (η) attention
πρόστιμο (το) fine
προσωπική κλίση person-to-person call
πρόχειρος/η/ο handy; impromptu ‖ πρόχειρο φαγητό snacks

Α	α	A
Β	β	V
Γ	γ	G
Δ	δ	D
Ε	ε	E
Ζ	ζ	Z
Η	η	I
Θ	θ	Th
Ι	ι	I
Κ	κ	K
Λ	λ	L
Μ	μ	M
Ν	ν	N
Ξ	ξ	X
Ο	ο	O
Π	π	P
Ρ	ρ	R
Σ	σ,ς	S
Τ	τ	T
Υ	υ	I
Φ	φ	F
Χ	χ	H
Ψ	ψ	Ps
Ω	ω	O

πρωί (το) morning
πρωινός/ή/ό morning || το πρωινό breakfast
πρωτεύουσα (η) capital city
πρωτομαγιά (η) May Day
πρώτος/η/ο first || πρώτες βοήθειες first aid || πρώτη θέση first class
πρωτοχρονιά (η) New Year's Day
πτήση (η) flight || πτήσεις εξωτερικού international flights || πτήσεις εσωτερικού domestic flights || αριθμός πτήσης flight number || ναυλωμένη πτήση charter flight || τακτικές πτήσεις scheduled flights
πυρκαγιά (η) fire
πυροσβεστήρας (ο) fire extinguisher
πυροσβέστης (ο) fireman
πυροσβεστική (η) fire brigade || πυροσβεστική υπηρεσία fire brigade || πυροσβεστική φωλεά case where fire-fighting equipment is kept || πυροσβεστικός σταθμός fire station
πώληση (η) sale || λιανική πώληση retail sale || χονδρική πώληση wholesale
πωλητής/τρια sales assistant || αυτόματος πωλητής γραμματοσήμων stamp machine
πωλώ to sell || πωλείται, πωλούνται for sale
πώς; how?

ρεζέρβα (η) spare wheel
ρέστα (τα) change *(money)*
ρετσίνα (η) retsina *(resinated white wine)*
ρεύμα (το) current
ρόδα (η) wheel
ροδάκινο (το) peach
ρόδι (το) pomegranate
Ροδίτικο a red wine from Rhodes
Ρόδος (η) Rhodes
ρολόι (το) watch; clock
Ρομπόλα a dry wine from Kefallonia
ρούμι (το) rum
ρύζι (το) rice

Α	α	A
Β	β	V
Γ	γ	G
Δ	δ	D
Ε	ε	E
Ζ	ζ	Z
Η	η	I
Θ	θ	Th
Ι	ι	I
Κ	κ	K
Λ	λ	L
Μ	μ	M
Ν	ν	N
Ξ	ξ	X
Ο	ο	O
Π	π	P
Ρ	ρ	R
Σ	σ,ς	S
Τ	τ	T
Υ	υ	I
Φ	φ	F
Χ	χ	H
Ψ	ψ	Ps
Ω	ω	O

ρυμουλκώ to tow away
Ροτόντα a red wine

Σάββατο (το) Saturday
Σαββατοκύριακο (το) weekend
σακκάκι (το) jacket
σάκχαρη (η) sugar
σαλάμι (το) salami
σαλάτα (η) salad
σαλιγκάρι (το) snail
σάλτσα (η) sauce
Σάμος (η) Samos *(island)* || Σάμος a sweet red wine
from Samos
σαμπάνια (η) champagne
σαμπουάν (το) shampoo
σάντουιτς (το) sandwich
σαπούνι (το) soap
σβήνω to extinguish; switch off || σβήσατε τα τσιγάρα
σας put out your cigarettes
Σεπτέμβριος (ο) September
σέρβις (το) service || ιδιωτικό σέρβις executive service
|| σέρβις ελαστικών tyre service
σεφ (ο) chef
σήμα (το) sign; signal || σήμα κατατεθέν trade mark ||
σήμα κινδύνου emergency signal || σήμα στον οδηγό
signal to the driver *(to stop)*
σήμερα today
σιγά slowly
σιγή (η) silence
σιδηρόδρομος (ο) train; railway || σιδηροδρομικός
σταθμός railway station || σιδηροδρομικώς by rail
σιεφταλιά (η) spicy minced-meat kebab
σκάλα (η) ladder; staircase
σκαλί (το) step
σκάφος (το) vessel || στο σκάφος on board || σκάφη
ανοιχτής θαλάσσης vessels for open sea || φουσκωτά
σκάφη inflatable boats

A	α	A
B	β	V
Γ	γ	G
Δ	δ	D
E	ε	E
Z	ζ	Z
H	η	I
Θ	θ	Th
I	ι	I
K	κ	K
Λ	λ	L
M	μ	M
N	ν	N
Ξ	ξ	X
O	ο	O
Π	π	P
P	ρ	R
Σ	σ,ς	S
T	τ	T
Υ	υ	I
Φ	φ	F
X	χ	H
Ψ	ψ	Ps
Ω	ω	O

σκέτος/η/ο plain || **ένας καφές σκέτος** coffee without sugar || **ένα σκέτο ουίσκυ** neat whisky

σκηνή (η) tent; stage

σκι ski || **θαλάσσιο σκι** water-ski(ing)

σκοινί (το) rope

σκορδαλιά (η) garlic sauce

σκόρδος (ο) garlic

σκουπίδι (το) rubbish; refuse

σκυλί (το) dog

Σκωτία (η) Scotland

σόδα (η) soda

σοκολάτα (η) chocolate

σόλα (η) sole *(of shoe)*

σολομός (ο) salmon

σόμπα (η) heater

σούβλα (η) skewer; lamb cooked on a skewer over charcoal

σουβλάκι (το) kebab

σούπα (η) soup

σουπεραγορά (η) supermarket

σπανάκι (το) spinach

σπανακόπιτα (η) spinach pie

σπαράγγι (το) asparagus

σπεσιαλιτέ της κουζίνας today's special dish

σπίρτο (το) match

σπίτι (το) house

σπορ (τα) sports

σπρώξτε push

στάδιο (το) stadium

σταθμαρχείο (το) stationmaster

στάθμευση/σις (η) parking || **στάθμευση αυτοκινήτων** car parking || **στάθευσις επί καταβολή τέλους** parking meters || **ανώτατος χρόνος σταθμεύσεως** maximum parking time || **απαγορεύεται η στάθμευση** no parking || **μη σταθμεύετε** no parking || **χώρος σταθμεύσεως** parking area

σταθμός (ο) station || **πυροσβεστικός σταθμός** fire

Α	α	A
Β	β	V
Γ	γ	G
Δ	δ	D
Ε	ε	E
Ζ	ζ	Z
Η	η	I
Θ	θ	Th
Ι	ι	I
Κ	κ	K
Λ	λ	L
Μ	μ	M
Ν	ν	N
Ξ	ξ	X
Ο	ο	O
Π	π	P
Ρ	ρ	R
Σ	σ,ς	S
Τ	τ	T
Υ	υ	I
Φ	φ	F
Χ	χ	H
Ψ	ψ	Ps
Ω	ω	O

station || σιδηροδρομικός σταθμός railway station
στάση/σις (η) stop || στάση εργασίας strike || στάσις ΗΛΠΑΠ trolley bus stop || στάση λεωφορείου bus stop
σταυροδρόμι (το) crossroads
σταφίδα (η) raisin
σταφύλι (το) grapes
στεγνοκαθαριστήριο (το) dry-cleaner's
στένωμα οδοστρώματος bottleneck
στιγμή (η) moment || μια στιγμή just a moment
στιγμιαίος καφές (ο) instant coffee
στιφάδο (το) beef stew with onions
στοά (η) arcade
στροφή (η) turn
στρώμα (το) mattress
συγγνώμη sorry
συγκοινωνία (η) transport
συγχαρητήρια congratulations
συγχωρώ: με συγχωρείτε excuse me
σύζυγος (ο/η) husband/wife
σύκο (το) fig
συκώτι (το) liver
συμπεριλαμβάνω to include || συμπεριλαμβανομένων φόρων και ποσοστού υπηρεσίας including taxes and service charge
συμπλέκτης (ο) clutch (of car)
συμπληρώνω to fill in
σύμπτωμα (το) symptom
συμφωνία (η) agreement
συνάλλαγμα (το) foreign exchange || δήλωση συναλλάγματος currency declaration || η τιμή του συναλλάγματος rate of foreign exchange
συνάντηση (η) meeting
συναυλία (η) concert
συνεργείο (το) workshop || συνεργείο αυτοκινήτων car repairs
σύνθεση (η) ingredients
σύνολο (το) total

A	α	A
B	β	V
Γ	γ	G
Δ	δ	D
E	ε	E
Z	ζ	Z
H	η	I
Θ	θ	Th
I	ι	I
K	κ	K
Λ	λ	L
M	μ	M
N	ν	N
Ξ	ξ	X
O	o	O
Π	π	P
P	ρ	R
Σ	σ,ς	S
T	τ	T
Υ	υ	I
Φ	φ	F
X	χ	H
Ψ	ψ	Ps
Ω	ω	O

σύνορα (τα) border; frontier

συνταγή (η) doctor's prescription; recipe

σύνταγμα (το) constitution ‖ Πλατεία Συντάγματος Constitution Square *(in Athens)*

συντηρητικά (τα) preservatives

σύρατε pull

σύστημα κλιματισμού air conditioning

συστημένη επιστολή registered letter

συχνά often

σφράγισμα (το) filling *(in tooth)*

σχηματίζω to form ‖ σχηματίστε τον αριθμό dial the number

σχολείο (το) school

σχολή (η) school ‖ σχολή οδηγών driving school

σώμα (το) body

σωσίβιο (το) life jacket ‖ ατομικό σωσίβιο personal life jacket ‖ παιδικά σωσίβια children's life jackets

σωφέρ (ο) chauffeur

ταβέρνα (η) tavern

τάβλι (το) backgammon

ταινία (η) film; strip; tape

ταμείο (το) cashier's desk; till

ταμίας (ο/η) cashier

ταμιευτήριο (το) savings bank

ταξί (το) taxi ‖ αγοραίο ταξί without a meter, fare to be agreed ‖ γραφείο ταξί taxi office ‖ ταξί ενοικιάζονται - πωλούνται taxis – for hire and for sale

ταξίδι (το) journey; tour ‖ καλό ταξίδι bon voyage ‖ ταξιδιωτικό γραφείο travel agent ‖ οργανωμένα ταξίδια organized tours ‖ πρακτορείο ταξιδίων travel agent

ταξιθέτης/τρια theatre attendant

ταραμοσαλάτα (η) taramosalata *(dish containing roe, often served as a starter)*

ταυτότητα (η) identity

ταχεία (η) express train

ταχυδρομείο (το) post office ‖ Ελληνικά Ταχυδρομεία Greek Post Office

Α	α	A
Β	β	V
Γ	γ	G
Δ	δ	D
Ε	ε	E
Ζ	ζ	Z
Η	η	I
Θ	θ	Th
Ι	ι	I
Κ	κ	K
Λ	λ	L
Μ	μ	M
Ν	ν	N
Ξ	ξ	X
Ο	ο	O
Π	π	P
Ρ	ρ	R
Σ	σ,ς	S
Τ	τ	T
Υ	υ	I
Φ	φ	F
Χ	χ	H
Ψ	ψ	Ps
Ω	ω	O

ταχυδρομικά (τέλη) postage || ταχυδρομικές επιταγές postal orders || ταχυδρομικός κώδικας postcode || ταχυδρομικώς by post

ταχύμετρο (το) speedometer

ταχύτητα/ταχύτης (η) speed || η ταχύτης ελέγχεται με ραντάρ radar speed check || κιβώτιο ταχύτητων gearbox

τέιον (το) tea

τελευταίος/α/ο last

τέλος (το) end; tax; duty || ταχυδρομικά τέλη postage || τέλος απηγορευμένης ζώνης end of no-overtaking zone

τελωνείο (το) customs

τέννις (το) tennis

τέντα (η) tent

τέρμα (το) terminus

τέρμιναλ (το) terminal

τέσσερα four (with neuter nouns)

τέσσερεις four (with masc. and fem. nouns)

Τετάρτη Wednesday

τέχνη (η) art || λαϊκή τέχνη folk art

τεχνητώς κεχρωσμένο contains artificial colourings

τζαμί (το) mosque

τηγανίτα (η) pancake

τηλεγραφείο (το) telegraph office

τηλεγράφημα (το) telegram

τηλεόραση (η) television

τηλεπικοινωνίες (οι) telecommunications || Οργανισμός Τηλεπικοινωνιών Ελλάδος Greek Telecommunications Authority

τηλεφώνημα (το) telephone call

τηλέφωνο (το) telephone || τηλεφωνικός κατάλογος telephone directory || τηλεφωνικός κώδικας dialling code || υπεραστικά τηλέφωνα telephones for long-distance calls

τι; what? || τι είναι; what is it?

τιμή (η) price; honour || τιμή εισιτηρίου price of ticket; fare

τιμοκατάλογος (ο) price list

Α	α	A
Β	β	V
Γ	γ	G
Δ	δ	D
Ε	ε	E
Ζ	ζ	Z
Η	η	I
Θ	θ	Th
Ι	ι	I
Κ	κ	K
Λ	λ	L
Μ	μ	M
Ν	ν	N
Ξ	ξ	X
Ο	ο	O
Π	π	P
Ρ	ρ	R
Σ	σ,ς	S
Τ	τ	T
Υ	υ	I
Φ	φ	F
Χ	χ	H
Ψ	ψ	Ps
Ω	ω	O

τιμολόγιο (το) invoice
τιμόνι (το) steering wheel
τιμωρώ to punish ‖ πάσα ζημιά τιμωρείται με φυλάκιση anyone causing damage will be prosecuted
τίποτα nothing
τμήμα (το) department; police station
το it; the (with neuter nouns)
τοιχοκόλληση (η) bill posting
τόκος (o) interest (bank); τόκος καταθέσεων interest on deposits
τόνικ (το) tonic
τόνος (o) ton; tuna fish; tone of voice
τοοστ (το) toasted sandwich
τουαλέτα (η) bathroom; toilet
τουρισμός (o) tourism
τουρίστας/στρια tourist
τουριστικά: τουριστικά είδη souvenirs ‖ τουριστική αστυνομία Tourist Police
Τουρκία (η) Turkey
τραγούδι (το) song
τραγωδία (η) tragedy
τραίνο (το) train
τράπεζα (η) bank
τραπεζαρία (η) dining room
τραπέζι (το) table
τρεις three (with masc. and fem. nouns)
τρία three (with neuter nouns)
Τρίτη (η) Tuesday
τρίτος/η/ο third
τρόλλεϋ (το) trolley bus
τροφή (η) food
τροχαία (η) traffic police
τροχός (o) wheel
τροχόσπιτο (το) caravan
τροχοφόρο (το) vehicle
τρώγω/τρώω to eat
τσάι (το) tea

Α	α	A
Β	β	V
Γ	γ	G
Δ	δ	D
Ε	ε	E
Ζ	ζ	Z
Η	η	I
Θ	θ	Th
Ι	ι	I
Κ	κ	K
Λ	λ	L
Μ	μ	M
Ν	ν	N
Ξ	ξ	X
Ο	ο	O
Π	π	P
Ρ	ρ	R
Σ	σ,ς	S
Τ	τ	T
Υ	υ	I
Φ	φ	F
Χ	χ	H
Ψ	ψ	Ps
Ω	ω	O

τσάντα (η) bag
τσατσίκι (το) tsatsiki *(starter containing yoghurt, cucumber and garlic)*
τσιγάρο (το) cigarette
τυρί (το) cheese
τυρόπιτες (οι) cheese pies || τυρόπιτες σφολιάτα flaky pastry cheese pies
τυφλός/ή/ό blind

υάρδα (η) yard
υγεία (η) health || στην υγειά σας your health; cheers
υγειονομικός έλεγχος health inspection
Ύδρα (η) Hydra
υδραγωγείο (το) water reservoir
ύδωρ (το) water
Υμηττός (ο) Mount Hymettos || Υμηττός a dry red or white table wine from Athens
υπεραγορά (η) supermarket
υπεραστικό: υπεραστικό τηλεφώνημα long-distance call || υπεραστικό λεωφορείο long-distance coach
υπερωκεάνειο (το) liner
υπήκοος (ο/η) citizen
υπηκοότης/υπηκοότητα (η) nationality
υπηρεσία (η) service || Υπηρεσία φορτώσεως εμπορευμάτων cargo loading || ποσοστό υπηρεσίας service charge
υπηρέτης (ο) servant
υπηρέτρια (η) maid
υπόγειος/α/ο underground || υπόγεια διάβαση πεζών (pedestrian) subway || υπόγειος σιδηρόδρομος underground *(railway)*
υποδοχή (η) reception || χώρος υποδοχής reception area
υποκατάστημα (το) branch office
υπουργείο (το) ministry || Υπουργείο Πολιτισμού Ministry of Culture
υψηλός/ή/ό high || υψηλή τάση high voltage

A	α	A
B	β	V
Γ	γ	G
Δ	δ	D
E	ε	E
Z	ζ	Z
H	η	I
Θ	θ	Th
I	ι	I
K	κ	K
Λ	λ	L
M	μ	M
N	ν	N
Ξ	ξ	X
O	o	O
Π	π	P
P	ρ	R
Σ	σ,ς	S
T	τ	T
Υ	υ	I
Φ	φ	F
X	χ	H
Ψ	ψ	Ps
Ω	ω	O

ύφασμα (το) fabric; cloth ‖ **υφάσματα** textiles ‖ **υφάσματα επιπλώσεων** upholstery fabrics

ύψος (το) height ‖ **ύψος περιορισμένο** height limit

φαγητό (το) food

φαΐ (το) food

φακός (ο) lens ‖ **φακοί επαφής** contact lenses

φανός (ο) headlight

φαρμακείο (το) chemist's

φαρμάκι (το) poison

φάρμακο (το) medicine

φάρος (ο) lighthouse

φασολάδα (η) boiled haricot beans

φασολάκι (το) green bean

φασόλι (το) haricot bean

Φεβρουάριος (ο) February

φέρρυ μποτ ferry boat

φέτα (η) feta cheese; slice

φιλενάδα (η) girlfriend; mistress

φιλέτο (το) fillet of meat

φιλμ (το) film ‖ **εμφανίσεις φιλμ** film developing

φιλοδώρημα (το) tip ‖ **φιλοδώρημα περιποιητού** service charge

φιλοξενία (η) hospitality

φίλος/η friend

φίλτρο (το) filter ‖ **φίλτρο αέρος** air filter ‖ **φίλτρο βενζίνης** petrol filter ‖ **φίλτρο λαδιού** oil filter

φιστίκι (το) peanut ‖ **φιστίκια Αιγίνης** pistachio nuts

φλας (το) flash *(camera)*

φοιτητής/τρια student

φοιτητικό εισιτήριο student ticket or fare

φόρεμα (το) dress

φορολογημένα είδη duty-paid goods

φόρος (ο) tax ‖ **συμπεριλαμβανομένων φόρων** including taxes

φουντούκι (το) hazelnut

φούρνος (ο) oven

Α	α	A
Β	β	V
Γ	γ	G
Δ	δ	D
Ε	ε	E
Ζ	ζ	Z
Η	η	I
Θ	θ	Th
Ι	ι	I
Κ	κ	K
Λ	λ	L
Μ	μ	M
Ν	ν	N
Ξ	ξ	X
Ο	ο	O
Π	π	P
Ρ	ρ	R
Σ	σ,ς	S
Τ	τ	T
Υ	υ	I
Φ	φ	F
Χ	χ	H
Ψ	ψ	Ps
Ω	ω	O

φουρνάρικο (το) bakery
φουσκώνω: φουσκωτά σκάφη inflatable boats
φράουλα (η) strawberry
φρένα (τα) brakes *(in car)*
φρέσκος/ια/ο fresh
φρούτο (το) fruit
φρουτοσαλάτα (η) fruit salad
φρυγανιά (η) toast
φύλακας (ο) guard
φυτό (το) plant
φυτώριο (το) nursery *(for plants)*
φως (το) light
φωτιά (η) fire
φωτογραφία (η) photograph || **έγχρωμες φωτογραφίες** colour photographs
φωτογραφίζω to take photographs || **μη φωτογραφίζετε** no photographs
φωτογραφική μηχανή camera
φωτόμετρο (το) light meter
φωτοτυπία (η) photocopy

χαίρετε hello
χαίρομαι I am glad
χάπι (το) pill
χάρτης (ο) map || **οδικός χάρτης** road map
χαρτί (το) paper
χαρτικά (τα) stationery
χαρτονόμισμα (το) note *(money)* || **χαρτονομίσματα στην τρύπα** insert notes in the slot *(sign on fare machines, etc)*
χαρτοπωλείο stationer's shop
χαρτόσημο (το) stamp tax
χασάπης (ο) butcher
χασάπικο (το) butcher's shop
χειροποίητος/η/ο handmade
χειρούργος (ο) surgeon
χειρόφρενο (το) handbrake

Α	α	A
Β	β	V
Γ	γ	G
Δ	δ	D
Ε	ε	E
Ζ	ζ	Z
Η	η	I
Θ	θ	Th
Ι	ι	I
Κ	κ	K
Λ	λ	L
Μ	μ	M
Ν	ν	N
Ξ	ξ	X
Ο	ο	O
Π	π	P
Ρ	ρ	R
Σ	σ,ς	S
Τ	τ	T
Υ	υ	I
Φ	φ	F
Χ	χ	H
Ψ	ψ	Ps
Ω	ω	O

χέρι (το) hand

χιλιόμετρο (το) kilometre

χιόνι (το) snow

χοιρινό (το) pork

χονδρικός/ή/ό wholesale ΙΙ χονδρική πώληση wholesale

χορός (ο) dance

χορτοφαγία (η) vegetarianism

χορτοφάγος (ο/η) vegetarian

χορωδία (η) choir

χουρμάς (ο) date *(fruit)*

χρήματα (τα) money

χρηματοκιβώτιο (το) safe *(for valuables)*

χρηματοθυρίς (η) deposits; nightsafe *(bank)*

χρήση (η) use ΙΙ άσκοπη χρήση διώκεται ποινικώς improper use will lead to prosecution ΙΙ οδηγίες χρήσεως instructions for use

χριστιανός/ή Christian

Χριστούγεννα (τα) Christmas

χρόνος (ο) time; year

χρυσαφικά (τα) jewellery

χρυσός/ή/ό (made of) gold ΙΙ Χρυσός Οδηγός Yellow Pages

χτένα (η) comb

χτες yesterday

χύμα not bottled ΙΙ κρασί χύμα house wine

χυμός (ο) juice ΙΙ χυμός λεμονιού lemon juice ΙΙ χυμός πορτοκάλι orange juice

χώρα (η) country

χωριάτικη σαλάτα *see* **MENUS**

χωριάτικο ψωμί 'village' bread *(round, flat loaf)*

χωριό (το) village

χωρίς without ΙΙ χωρίς εισπράκτορα exact fare; no change given

χώρος (ο) area; site ΙΙ αρχαιολογικός χώρος archaeological site ΙΙ ιδιωτικός χώρος private ΙΙ χώρος αλιευτικών σκαφών for fishing boats only ΙΙ χώρος με απαγορευτική ένδειξη no smoking area ΙΙ χώρος

Α	α	A
Β	β	V
Γ	γ	G
Δ	δ	D
Ε	ε	E
Ζ	ζ	Z
Η	η	I
Θ	θ	Th
Ι	ι	I
Κ	κ	K
Λ	λ	L
Μ	μ	M
Ν	ν	N
Ξ	ξ	X
Ο	ο	O
Π	π	P
Ρ	ρ	R
Σ	σ,ς	S
Τ	τ	T
Υ	υ	I
Φ	φ	F
Χ	χ	H
Ψ	ψ	Ps
Ω	ω	O

αποσκευών car boot || **χώρος σταθμεύσεως** parking area
|| **χώρος υποδοχής** reception area

ψάρεμα (το) fishing
ψάρι (το) fish
ψαρόβαρκα (η) fishing boat
ψαρόσουπα (η) fish soup
ψαροταβέρνα (η) fish tavern
ψημένος/η/ο cooked
ψησταριά (η) rotisserie
ψητός/ή/ό roast
ψιλά (τα) small change
ψιλικά (τα) haberdashery
ψωμάκι (το) bread roll
ψωμάς (ο) baker
ψωμί (το) bread || **ψωμί χωριάτικο** 'village' bread

ωθήσατε push
ωτοστόπ (το) hitchhiking
ώρα (η) time || **ώρες εισόδου του κοινού** opening hours
for the public || **ώρες επισκέψεως** visiting hours ||
ώρες λειτουργίας opening hours || **ώρες περισυλλογής**
collection times || **ώρες συναλλαγής** banking hours ||
της ώρας freshly cooked *(food)*

Α	α	A
Β	β	V
Γ	γ	G
Δ	δ	D
Ε	ε	E
Ζ	ζ	Z
Η	η	I
Θ	θ	Th
Ι	ι	I
Κ	κ	K
Λ	λ	L
Μ	μ	M
Ν	ν	N
Ξ	ξ	X
Ο	ο	O
Π	π	P
Ρ	ρ	R
Σ	σ,ς	S
Τ	τ	T
Υ	υ	I
Φ	φ	F
Χ	χ	H
Ψ	ψ	Ps
Ω	ω	O